Welcome to the Everyday Instant Pot®! I have found my Instant Pot® to be a valuable kitchen appliance in preparing food that is not only quick and easy, but extremely tasty. It has helped me with the dreaded weeknight dinner scramble and has revolutionized the way I cook for my family. I found that we eat out less, we eat healthier foods more often and I have less stress in the kitchen. I love using this pressure cooker and I know you will, too!

My life can be hectic as I'm sure yours can be, too. I have 2 small girls and a menagerie of animals that take up a lot of my time. My husband likes to eat healthy, but doesn't have much kitchen sense. I am a bit of a foodie who expresses love through cooking. How do you combine all of that so that it works and everyone is happy? The Instant Pot® has been a big help in answering that question.

This book is a compilation of a variety of recipes that I have used in my kitchen. Some are great for that quick, easy meal and have simple ingredient lists. Others may require a bit more time and some more complex ingredients, but these special occasion dishes will blow you away. Many of these recipes are kid friendly and of course, most can be developed to fit your specific taste and dietary needs.

I tried to focus most of this book on main dishes, as I feel that is what most people search for. There is a wide variety of chicken, pork, beef and even seafood recipes here. I also included many pasta and side dishes to round out your cooking and dining experience. And finally, the dessert section will surely satisfy your sweet tooth and be a perfect complement to your everyday meals.

For even more recipes and fun giveaways, including an Instant Pot® giveaway, head over to mamaunderpressure.com!

BENEFITS OF COOKING WITH THE INSTANT POT® PRESSURE COOKER

The Instant Pot® programmable pressure cooker is probably the most amazing machine in my kitchen, maybe any kitchen. It's so convenient due to the wide selection of cooking functions such as pressure cooking, slow cooking, cooking rice and porridge, steaming, sautéing or browning, yogurt making, warming and diaper changing. Well, maybe not the diaper changing but a girl can dream! Seriously though, you name it and the Instant Pot® probably does it. With these cooking functions you can practically cook ANY type of dish.

The Instant Pot® also minimizes the preparation and cooking time by being one do-it-all appliance for sautéing, browning, boiling and simmering and of course, cooking. That means you'll spend less time washing dishes and cleaning the kitchen and more time doing the things you love. The cooking time is also reduced, great for busy chefs, and the amount of energy is minimized.

With the wide selection of cooking programs, you can cook dishes according to the consistency and texture that you prefer. Using the less/low mode, normal mode and more/high mode allows you to adjust cooking temperatures in preparing meals of various ingredient types. It also automatically adjusts pressure and temperature according to the volume of food for even and consistent cooking.

And it is VERY SAFE to use due to the safety lid lock that avoids accidental opening of the cooker when it is still at high pressure. The pressure and temperature is maintained in safe limits and it detects leaks if the lid is partially closed.

BASIC OPERATIONS KEYS

The "**+**" and "**-**" are used to adjust cooking time durations.

The **"adjust"** and **"pressure"** keys adjust high to low pressure cooking. It can also adjust "Soup", "Bean/Chili", "Poultry", "Meat/Stew", "Multigrain", "Porridge", "Steam", "Rice" and "Manual" functions.

PRESSURE COOKER FUNCTION KEYS

Keep **Warm/Cancel** Function
This is used to stop the cooking process when the pressure cooker is programmed and still in effect. It can also be used for keeping the food warm before serving.

The **Soup** Function
This is basically for cooking soup recipes and can adjust cooking time duration using the adjust button.

The **Porridge** Function
This is used for cooking porridge of different grains. For basic rice porridge adjust to less and for a mixture of varied rice porridges use more. Do not position the steam release handle when the cooking cycle has been completed because it might splash out liquid from the pressure cooker.

The **Poultry** Function
This function is used for various poultry dishes and can be adjusted to less, normal and more mode for texture preference.

The **Meat/Stew** Function
This is used for meat recipes and recipes with sauce ingredients. The cooking time can be adjusted for texture preference of the meat.

The **Bean/Chili** Function
This function is specially used for recipes with beans and can be adjusted to less and more modes for texture preference.

The **Rice** Function
This function is used to cook rice with automatic pressure and temperature control. The cooking duration is also automatically adjusted depending on the volume of food in the pot.

The **Multigrain** Function
This function is used specifically for cooking mixed grain varieties. It can be adjusted to less, normal and more mode. More mode has 45 minutes of soaking time in the warm setting and up to 60 minutes of pressure cooking time.

The **Steam** Function
This cooking function is specially designed for steaming different ingredient types. Please see the cooking time tables for exact cooking time and temperatures in cooking various food types.

The **Manual** Function
With this cooking function, pressure cooking time can be manually adjusted up to 120 minutes with maximum amount of pressure.

The **Sauté** Function
This special cooking function allows you to sauté ingredients and brown meats in preparation for cooking different dishes such as soups and stews, beans and chilli and any other dishes that are prepared with sautéing.

The **Slow Cook** Function
This function makes the Instant Pot® incredibly versatile as it turns your pressure cooker into a slow cooker with adjustable temperature controls.

The **Yogurt** Function
This function has adjustable modes from low, normal and more for preparing yogurt and pasteurizing milk.

The **Timer** Function
This function is also called the delay timer which is used in soaking ingredients before cooking. This is also for preparing dishes ahead in the pressure cooker if you want exact timing in serving dishes according to adjusted time.

PRESSURE COOKING TIME TABLES

MEAT (POULTRY, BEEF, PORK AND LAMB)

Meat Types	Cooking Time (in Minutes)
Beef, stew meat	15 to 20
Beef, meat ball	10 to 15
Beef, dressed	20 to 25
Beef, pot roast, steak, rump, round, chuck, blade or brisket, large	35 to 40
Beef, pot roast, steak, rump, round, chuck, blade or brisket, small chunks	25 to 30
Beef, ribs	25 to 30
Beef, shanks	25 to 30
Beef, oxtail	40 to 50
Chicken, breasts	8 to 10
Chicken, whole	20 to 25
Chicken, cut up with bones	10 to 15
Chicken, dark meat	10 to 15
Cornish Hen, whole	10 to 15
Duck, cut up with bones	10 to 12
Duck, whole	25 to 30
Pheasant	20 to 25
Turkey, breast, boneless	15 to 20
Turkey, breast, whole, with bones	25 to 30
Turkey, drumsticks (leg)	15 to 20
Quail, whole	8 to 10
Lamb, cubes	10 to15
Lamb, stew meat	10 to 15
Lamb, leg	35 to 45
Ham slice	9 to 12
Ham picnic shoulder	25 to 30
Pork, loin roast	55 to 60
Pork, butt roast	45 to 50

Meat Types	Cooking Time (in Minutes)
Pork, ribs	20 to 25
Veal, chops	5 to 8
Veal, roast	35 to 45

SEAFOOD AND FISH

Fish and Seafood Types	Cooking Time in Minutes (Fresh)	Cooking Time in Minutes (Frozen)
Crab	3 to 4	5 to 6
Fish, whole	5 to 6	7 to 10
Fish fillet	2 to 3	3 to 4
Fish steak	3 to 4	4 to 6
Lobster	3 to 4	4 to 6
Mussels	2 to 3	4 to 5
Seafood soup or stock	6 to 7	7 to 9
Shrimp or Prawn	1 to 2	2 to 3

RICE AND GRAINS

Rice & Grain Varieties	Water Quantity (Grain : Water ratios)	Cooking Time (in Minutes)
Barley, pearl	1:4	25 to 30
Barley, pot	1:3 ~ 1:4	25 to 30
Congee, thick	1:4 ~ 1:5	15 to 20
Congee, thin	1:6 ~ 1:7	15 to 20
Couscous	1:2	5 to 8
Corn, dried, half	1:3	25 to 30
Kamut, whole	1:3	10 to 12
Millet	1:1 2/3	10 to 12
Oats, quick cooking	1:1	6
Oats, steel cut	1:1 2/3	10
Porridge, thin	1:6 ~ 1:7	15 to 20
Quinoa, quick cooking	1:2	8
Rice, Basmati	1: 1.5	4 to 8
Rice, Brown	1: 1.25	22 to 28
Rice, Jasmine	1: 1	4 to 10

Rice & Grain Varieties	Water Quantity (Grain : Water ratios)	Cooking Time (in Minutes)
Rice, white	1: 1.5	8
Rice, wild	1:3	25 to 30
Sorghum	1:3	20 to 25
Spelt berries	1:3	15 to 20
Wheat berries	1:3	25 to 30

FRESH OR FROZEN VEGETABLE

Vegetable Types	Cooking Time in Minutes (Fresh)	Cooking Time in Minutes (Frozen)
Artichoke, whole, trimmed without leaves	9 to 11	11 to 13
Artichoke, hearts	4 to 5	5 to 6
Asparagus, whole or cut	1 to 2	2 to 3
Beans, green/yellow or wax, whole, trim ends and strings	1 to 2	2 to 3
Beets, small roots, whole	11 to 13	13 to 15
Beets, large roots, whole	20 to 25	25 to 30
Broccoli, flowerets	2 to 3	3 to 4
Broccoli, stalks	3 to 4	4 to 5
Brussel sprouts, whole	3 to 4	4 to 5
Cabbage, red, purple or green, shredded	2 to 3	3 to 4
Cabbage, red, purple or green, wedges	3 to 4	4 to 5
Carrots, sliced or shredded	1 to 2	2 to 3
Carrots, whole or chunked	2 to 3	3 to 4
Cauliflower flowerets	2 to 3	3 to 4
Celery, chunks	2 to 3	3 to 4
Collard	4 to 5	5 to 6
Corn, kernels	1 to 2	2 to 3
Corn, on the cob	3 to 4	4 to 5
Eggplant, slices or chunks	2 to 3	3 to 4
Endive	1 to 2	2 to 3
Escarole, chopped	1 to 2	2 to 3
Green beans, whole	2 to 3	3 to 4

Vegetable Types	Cooking Time in Minutes (Fresh)	Cooking Time in Minutes (Frozen)
Greens(beet greens, collards, kale, spinach, swiss chard, turnip greens), chopped	3 to 6	4 to 7
Leeks	2 to 4	3 to 5
Mixed vegetables	2 to 3	3 to 4
Okra	2 to 3	3 to 4
Onions, sliced	2 to 3	3 to 4
Parsnips, sliced	1 to 2	2 to 3
Parsnips, chunks	2 to 4	4 to 6
Peas, in the pod	1 to 2	2 to 3
Peas, green	1 to 2	2 to 3
Potatoes, in cubes	7 to 9	9 to 11
Potatoes, whole, baby	10 to 12	12 to 14
Potatoes, whole, large	12 to 15	15 to 19
Pumpkin, small slices or chunks	4 to 5	6 to 7
Pumpkin, large slices or chunks	8 to 10	10 to 14
Rutabaga, slices	3 to 5	4 to 6
Rutabaga, chunks	4 to 6	6 to 8
Spinach	1 to 2	3 to 4
Squash, acorn, slices or chunks	6 to 7	8 to 9
Squash, butternut, slices or chunks	8 to 10	10 to 12
Sweet potato, in cubes	7 to 9	9 to 11
Sweet potato, whole, small	10 to 12	12 to 14
Sweet potato, whole, large	12 to 15	15 to 19
Sweet pepper, slices or chunks	1 to 3	2 to 4
Tomatoes, in quarters	2 to 3	4 to 5

DRIED BEANS, LEGUME AND LENTILS

Dried Beans & Legume Types	Cooking Time in Minutes (Dry)	Cooking Time in Minutes (Soaked)
Adzuki	20 to 25	10 to 15
Anasazi	20 to 25	10 to 15
Black beans	20 to 25	10 to 15
Black eyed peas	20 to 25	10 to 15
Chickpeas (chick peas, garbanzo bean or kabuli)	35 to 40	20 to 25

Dried Beans & Legume Types	Cooking Time in Minutes (Dry)	Cooking Time in Minutes (Soaked)
Cannellini beans	35 to 40	20 to 25
Gandules (pigeon peas)	20 to 25	15 to 20
Great Northern beans	25 to 30	20 to 25
Lentils, French green	15 to 20	N/A
Lentils, green, mini (brown)	15 to 20	N/A
Lentils, red, split	15 to 18	N/A
Lentils, yellow, split (moong dal)	15 to 18	N/A
Lima beans	20 to 25	10 to 15
Kidney beans, red	25 to 30	20 to 25
Kidney beans, white	35 to 40	20 to 25
Navy beans	25 to 30	20 to 25
Pinto beans	25 to 30	20 to 25
Peas	15 to 20	10 to 15
Scarlet runner	20 to 25	10 to 15
Soy beans	25 to 30	20 to 25

FRUITS

Fruit Types	Cooking Time in Minutes (Fresh)	Cooking Time in Minutes (Dried)
Apples, in slices or pieces	2 to 3	3 to 4
Apples, whole	3 to 4	4 to 6
Apricots, whole or halves	2 to 3	3 to 4
Peaches	2 to 3	4 to 5
Pears, whole	3 to 4	4 to 6
Pears, slices or halves	2 to 3	4 to 5
Prunes	2 to 3	4 to 5
Raisins	N/A	4 to 5

TABLE OF CONTENTS

Soups and Stews 17
- BLACK BEAN SOUP 19
- CREAMY TOMATO BASIL PARMESAN SOUP 21
- SPLIT PEA AND HAM SOUP 23
- CHEESY BROCCOLI SOUP 25
- LENTIL SOUP 27
- BEEFY NOODLE SOUP 28
- FENNEL SOUP 30
- SEAFOOD CORN CHOWDER 31
- CHICKEN ORZO SOUP 32
- FISHERMAN'S SEAFOOD CHOWDER 33
- CLAM CHOWDER 34
- YELLOW SPLIT-PEA SOUP WITH KALE AND POTATOES 37
- BLACK BEAN SOUP WITH AVOCADO SALSA ... 38
- TURKEY, SWEET POTATO AND BLACK BEAN CHILI 40
- PORK AND HOMINY STEW 41
- CREAMY POTATO SOUP 43
- EASY BEEF STEW 45
- CHICKEN NOODLE SOUP 47

Pork 49
- PEPPERED SWEET PORK RIBS 50
- PORK CHOPS WITH CABBAGE 51
- PULLED PORK 52
- JAPANESE PORK BELLY 54
- PORK WITH TOMATOES 56
- HONEY-GARLIC PORK RIBS 59
- PORK SHOULDER 60
- PORK LOIN 61
- PORK TENDERLOIN 63
- PORK ROAST 64
- CREAMY TENDER PORK CHOPS 65
- VEGETABLES AND PORK CHOPS 66
- PORK CHOP WITH SAUERKRAUT 67
- RED BEANS AND PORK CHOPS 68
- ROASTED PORK WITH FENNEL 70

Beef 71
- BBQ BEEF SHORT RIBS 73
- BEEF BOURGUIGNON 75
- ONION-MUSHROOMS BEEF TIPS 76
- BRAISED BEEF SHANKS 77
- POT ROAST 79
- BEEF STROGANOFF 81
- BEEF TENDERLOIN IN MUSHROOM SAUCE 83
- TEX MEX BRISKET 85
- BEEF IN MOCHA SAUCE 86
- MEXICAN BEEF RECIPE 87
- BEEF SHORT RIBS WITH MASHED VEGETABLES 88
- MONGOLIAN BEEF 91
- CHILI BEEF BURRITOS 93

Poultry 95
- CHICKEN CACCIATORE 97
- TURKEY WITH ORANGE-WHISKEY SAUCE 98
- TURKEY BREAST IN ORANGE-CRANBERRY SAUCE 99
- SEASONED WHOLE CHICKEN 101
- CHICKEN THIGHS 103
- THAI CHICKEN THIGHS 104
- GREEN CHILE WITH CHICKEN 105
- CHICKEN AND CHICKPEA MASALA 107
- HAWAIIAN BBQ CHICKEN 108
- CHICKEN A LA KING 109
- CHICKEN WITH SHERRY, MUSTARD & OLIVES 111

14 | Everyday Instant Pot®

TURKEY WITH GRAVY...................................113
CHICKEN WITH CHORIZO AND
CHICKPEAS IN TOMATO SAUCE 114
CHICKEN THIGHS WITH
ARTICHOKES...115
SMOKED PAPRIKA
MARINATED CHICKEN 116

Seafood............................117
NEW ORLEANS STYLE
BARBECUE SHRIMP..119
CITRUS PRAWN & PEA RISOTTO 121
SHRIMP SCAMPI 122
CALAMARI IN TOMATO SAUCE 123
TILAPIA WITH
ORANGE-GINGER SAUCE 125
COCONUT FISH CURRY 127
SHRIMP ETOUFFEE 129
LOBSTER TAILS 130
COD WITH PEAS IN PESTO SAUCE 131
SALMON IN WHITE WINE 133
MUSTARD SALMON 134
LOW COUNTRY SHRIMP BOIL 135
SALMON AND VEGGIES 137

Rice and Pasta...................139
BROWN RICE 141
ONE POT SPAGHETTI......................................143
BOLOGNESE RAGU PASTA SAUCE................144
RISOTTO 145
SPANISH RICE 146
CHICKEN ENCHILADA PASTA 147
MAC AND CHEESE 149
CHICKEN ALFREDO 151
ZITI WITH SAUSAGE 153

CHEESY CHICKEN AND
BROCCOLI WITH RICE....................................155
CHEESY MEATY PASTA..................................156
LENTILS AND RICE 157
MEXICAN RED RICE 159
MUSHROOM "RISOTTO"................................161

Vegetable and Side Dishes 163
GREEN BEANS AND BACON...........................165
BEER BRAISED CABBAGE WITH BACON......166
ARTICHOKES...167
SICILIAN STUFFED ARTICHOKES 168
PINTO BEANS 169
POTATOES AND GREEN BEANS....................171
ROASTED GARLIC...173
BEET & CAPER SALAD 174
COLLARD GREENS...175
CREAMY MASHED POTATOES 177
BOK CHOI OR CHINESE CABBAGE...............178
SOUTHERN CABBAGE...................................179
EGGPLANT WITH OLIVE SPREAD.................181
CHEESY ITALIAN POTATOES 183
TOMATO STEWED GREEN BEANS................184

Desserts 185
DULCE DE LECHE 187
PINA COLADA RICE PUDDING......................188
LEMON BLACKBERRY CUSTARDS................189
CHOCOLATE FONDUE 191
EASY HAZELNUT FLAN 192
BLUEBERRY PUDDING 193
CHEESECAKE 195
CREME BRULEE 197
FUDGY BROWNIES 199
LEMON CHEESECAKE...................................201

Soups and Stews

BLACK BEAN SOUP

This is a tasty, comforting soup that you can experiment with and change the flavors to please your own taste buds. By adding a variety of toppings you can completely change this dish. Tomatoes, peppers, avocado, cheese and sour cream are all great suggestions to add to this yummy soup.

Directions:

1. Add the oil into the inner pot of your Instant Pot®. Press the sauté key and adjust to normal mode. Once the oil is hot, add and sauté the onions, garlic, red pepper, bay leaf, oregano and cumin for about 5 minutes.
2. Add the soaked beans, vinegar, red wine, stock and season to taste with salt and pepper. Briefly stir the ingredients and close the lid securely. Rotate the lid clockwise approximately 30 degrees until the mark on the lid is aligned with the "Close" mark position. Position the steam release handle properly and align the pointed end of the steam release handle pointing to "Sealing", indicating that the Instant Pot® is in the sealed position. Press the "Bean/chili" button to start the cooking process.
3. When the cooking process is done, let the pressure release naturally and wait for 15 minutes before opening the lid, or until the floating valve has dropped. When the floating valve has dropped, carefully remove the lid by holding and turning it counter clockwise to the open position and lift it to open.
4. Portion the soup into individual serving bowls and serve warm with preferred toppings.

Ingredients:

- 2 cups of black beans (dried), soaked and drained
- 2 tablespoons of olive oil
- 2 medium purple onions, diced
- 1 medium red sweet pepper, diced
- 1 tablespoon of minced garlic
- 1 bay leaf
- ½ tablespoon of cumin powder
- ½ tablespoon of dried oregano leaves
- ½ tablespoon of crushed black pepper
- ½ tablespoon of salt
- 2 to 3 tablespoons of sherry vinegar
- 5 to 6 tablespoons of red wine
- 4 cups vegetable stock
- Red bell pepper, sliced or chopped, for serving
- Tomatoes slices, for serving
- Avocado slices, for serving
- Red onions, thinly sliced for serving
- Scallions, chopped for serving

Preparation time: 5 minutes
Cooking time: 25 minutes
Serves: 4-6

CREAMY TOMATO BASIL PARMESAN SOUP

This soup is always a hit in our house. It's creamy and comforting and best of all the kids gobble it up without me having to remind them. Truth be told, I didn't like tomato soup at all until recently. Now, I make this soup often, perhaps to make up for lost time! I recommend serving with grilled cheese.

Directions:

1. Add the butter into the inner pot. Press the sauté key and adjust to normal mode. When the butter has melted, add the onions, carrots and celery and sauté for about 10 minutes or until tender. Stir in the garlic, sauté for 1 minute and add the tomatoes, basil and stock. Season to taste with salt and pepper, and then briefly stir to combine. Close the lid securely.
2. Rotate the lid clockwise approximately 30 degrees until the mark on the lid is aligned with the "Close" mark position. Position the steam release handle properly and align the pointed end of the steam release handle pointing to "Sealing", indicating that the Instant Pot® is in the sealed position. Press the "Soup" button to start the cooking process.
3. When the cooking process is done, use the quick release method by sliding the steam handle to venting position until the pressure is fully released.
4. When the floating valve has dropped, carefully remove the lid. To open the lid, hold and turn it counter clockwise to the open position and lift it to open. Remove the inner pot from the pressure cooker and let it cool completely.
5. Transfer the soup into a food processor and puree until smooth. Return mixture in the pot and place the inner pot into the pressure cooker. Press the "Warm" button, add the cheese and cream and stir ingredients briefly. Close the lid and let it sit in the pressure cooker until ready for serving.

Ingredients:

- ¼ cup of butter
- 1 white onion, chopped
- 1 medium celery stalk, chopped
- 2 medium carrots, peeled and diced
- 1 teaspoon of minced garlic
- 2 cups of chicken stock or broth
- 4 cups canned tomatoes
- 1 sprig of fresh basil leaves
- 2 to 3 teaspoons of tomato paste
- Salt and crushed black pepper, to taste
- ½ cup of grated Parmesan cheese
- 1 cup cream

Preparation time: 10 minutes
Cooking time: 20 minutes
Serves: 8

SPLIT PEA AND HAM SOUP

I loved split pea soup as a child, but was typically served the Campbell's version. This soup is so easy to make in the pressure cooker and tastes so much better than anything canned. Peas are also full of protein, so this is a tasty way to add this healthy vegetable to your menu.

Directions:

1. Add all ingredients into the inner pot of the Instant Pot®. Season to taste with salt and pepper, and then briefly stir to combine. Close the lid securely.
2. Rotate the lid clockwise approximately 30 degrees until the mark on the lid is aligned with the "Close" mark position. Position the steam release handle properly and align the pointed end of the steam release handle pointing to "Sealing", indicating that the pressure cooker is in the sealed position. Press the "Soup" button to start the cooking process.
3. When the cooking process is done, let the pressure release naturally and wait for 15 minutes before opening the lid, or until the floating valve has dropped. When the floating valve has dropped, carefully remove the lid by holding and turning it counter clockwise to the open position and lift it to open.
4. Portion the soup into individual serving bowls and serve warm.

Ingredients:

- 1 pound of split peas (dried) (2 and 1/4 cups)
- 8 cups of vegetable stock
- 2 cups of ham chunks
- 1 large white onion, chopped
- 1 large carrot, peeled and diced
- 2 medium stalks of celery, chopped
- 1 tablespoon of dried thyme leaves
- Salt and ground white pepper, to taste

Preparation time: **10 minutes**
Cooking time: **30 minutes**
Serves: **6 to 8**

CHEESY BROCCOLI SOUP

I love soup. It's my all-time favorite thing to eat. And cheesy, creamy soups are right there in the front of the line. This soup is a cinch in the pressure cooker and tastes like you really put a lot of effort into it. If you like a soup with more texture and chunks of vegetables adjust the amount of soup you puree. If you like a soup with no chunks, puree all of the soup. Whatever you do, don't let another cold night go by without adding this gem to your menu!

Directions:

1. Add the butter into the inner pot of the Instant Pot®. Press the sauté key and adjust to normal mode. When the butter has melted, add the onions and sauté until tender. Add the garlic and stir for one minute. Toss in the carrot and allow it to simmer in the butter with the onion and garlic for a few minutes, stirring frequently to prevent sticking to the bottom of the inner pot.
2. Add the broccoli and stock into the inner pot and close the lid securely.
3. Rotate the lid clockwise approximately 30 degrees until the mark on the lid is aligned with the "Close" mark position. Position the steam release handle properly and align the pointed end of the steam release handle pointing to "Sealing", indicating that your Instant Pot® is in the sealed position. Press the "Soup" button to start the cooking process.
4. When the cooking process is done, use the quick release method by sliding the steam handle to venting position until the pressure is fully released.
5. When the floating valve has dropped, carefully remove the lid. To open the lid, hold and turn it counter clockwise to the open position and lift it to open. Remove the inner pot from the pressure cooker and let it cool completely.
6. Transfer approximately half of the soup into a food processor and puree until smooth. Return mixture to the pot and place the inner pot into the pressure cooker. Press the "Warm" button and add the cheese, milk and cream. Season to taste with salt and pepper, and then stir ingredients briefly. Close the lid and let it sit in the pressure cooker until ready for serving.

Ingredients:

- 2 tablespoons of unsalted butter
- 2 garlic cloves, minced
- 1 small onion, chopped
- 1 small carrot, finely sliced
- 5 cups of detached broccoli florets
- 5 -6 cups of chicken stock
- 1 to 1 ½ cups of milk (1 cup if using the cream)
- 1/2 cup heavy cream (optional, but recommended)
- 2 cups of Cheddar cheese, shredded
- Salt and ground black pepper, to taste

Preparation time: 10 minutes
Cooking time: 20 minutes
Serves: 8

LENTIL SOUP

My husband loves to eat healthy so this soup is one he requests often. Lentils are extremely healthy, full of protein and fiber that make them a heart healthy choice. There are so many great vegetable textures in this soup that you won't miss the meat, but if you just can't live without it, try adding some diced ham when you stir in the leafy greens.

Directions:

1. Add the oil into the inner pot of the Instant Pot®. Press the sauté key and adjust to normal mode. Once the oil is hot, add the onions and garlic and sauté until soft and tender. Stir in potatoes, carrots, celery, cumin and paprika and sauté until the vegetables are tender. Add the remaining ingredients except for the leafy greens and season with salt and pepper.
2. Briefly stir the ingredients and close the lid securely. Rotate the lid clockwise approximately 30 degrees until the mark on the lid is aligned with the "Close" mark position. Position the steam release handle properly and align the pointed end of the steam release handle pointing to "Sealing", indicating that the pressure cooker is in the sealed position. Press the "Soup" button to start the cooking process.
3. When the cooking process is done, let the pressure release naturally and wait for 15 minutes before opening the lid, or until the floating valve has dropped. When the floating valve has dropped, carefully remove the lid by holding and turning it counter clockwise to the open position and lift it to open.
4. Stir in the leafy greens, press the "Warm" button and close the lid. Maintain keep warm mode before serving, or until the leafy vegetables are wilted. Adjust seasoning if desired.

Ingredients:

- 2 cups of lentils (red or green), rinsed and drained
- 1 red onion, diced
- 2 tablespoons of olive oil
- 2 teaspoons of minced garlic
- ½ tablespoon of ground cumin
- ½ to 1 tablespoon of paprika
- Salt and crushed black pepper, to taste
- 1 large carrot, peeled and halved lengthwise, sliced into ¼-inch thick pieces
- 2 medium stalks of celery, chopped
- 2 cups of diced potatoes (any variety)
- 1 cup loosely packed leafy greens, roughly chopped
- 8 cups of vegetable or chicken stock
- Salt and ground black pepper, to taste

Preparation time: 5 minutes
Cooking time: 20 minutes
Serves: 6

BEEFY NOODLE SOUP

This is a great soup that would be really impressive to serve as a starter when having guests for dinner. All of the spices make this soup really delicious.

Directions:

1. Add 1 tablespoon of oil into the inner pot of your Instant Pot®. Press the sauté key and adjust to normal mode. When the oil is hot, add the onions and ginger and sauté until lightly brown and aromatic. Remove from the pressure cooker, transfer onto a plate and set aside.
2. Add the remaining oil into the inner pot and switch the pressure cooker into "more" mode for browning the meats. Brown the meat in separate batches to sear them evenly. Add water just to cover the meat, and add the spice sachet and sautéed ingredients and then close the lid securely.
3. Rotate the lid clockwise approximately 30 degrees until the mark on the lid is aligned with the "Close" mark position. Position the steam release handle properly and align the pointed end of the steam release handle pointing to "Sealing", indicating that the pressure cooker is in the sealed position. Press the "Soup" button to start the cooking process.
4. When the cooking process is done, use the quick release method by sliding the steam handle to venting position until the pressure is fully released.
5. When the floating valve has dropped, carefully remove the lid. To open the lid, hold and turn it counter clockwise to the open position and lift it to open. Remove the beef from the inner pot, shred with two forks and place it in a plate. Remove the spice sachet and other ingredient, discard the spice sachet.
6. Pour in 4 cups of water, adjust taste by adding fish sauce and return the broth to a simmer. Switch to "Warm" mode to keep it warm before serving.
7. Portion the cooked noodles, shredded meat and roasted round eye slices into individual serving bowls and top with preferred garnishes. Pour in warm broth and serve immediately.

Preparation time: 15 minutes
Cooking time: 2 hours
Serves: 6

Ingredients:

- 2 tablespoons of olive oil
- 1 1-inch piece of fresh ginger root, sliced into ½-inch thick rounds
- 1 medium white onion, diced
- 1 pound of beef brisket, shredded
- 3 to 4 tablespoons of fish sauce
- 8 cups of fresh noodles, cooked ahead
- Water, as needed to cover the meat in the inner pot
- 4 cups water, for diluting the cooking liquid

For the Spice Sachet

- 2 star anise seeds, toasted
- 2 tablespoons whole seeds of coriander, toasted
- 1 3-inch stick of cinnamon, toasted
- 3 to 4 cloves. toasted
- 2 green pods of cardamom, toasted

For Serving

- 1 pound roasted beef eye round, sliced into thin pieces
- Fresh lime wedges
- Sliced jalapeño peppers
- Chopped fresh cilantro leaves
- Chopped fresh basil leaves
- Fresh mint leaves
- Fresh Bean sprouts
- Hot chili sauce

FENNEL SOUP

I've found fennel is a vegetable that some people have strong feelings about. If you like the taste of fennel, you will be excited to add this soup to your menu. It's easy to prepare and the leeks pair well with the fennel without trying to steal the show.

Directions:

1. Add all ingredients except the cheese into the inner pot of the pressure cooker. Adjust to soup mode and close the lid securely. Rotate the lid clockwise approximately 30 degrees until the mark on the lid is aligned with the "Close" mark position. Position the steam release handle properly and align the pointed end of the steam release handle pointing to "Sealing", indicating that the Instant Pot® is in the sealed position. Press the "Soup" button to start the cooking process.
2. When the cooking process is done, use the quick release method by sliding the steam handle to venting position until the pressure is fully released.
3. When the floating valve has dropped, carefully remove the lid. To open the lid, hold and turn it counter clockwise to the open position and lift it to open.
4. Portion fennel soup into individual serving bowls, serve warm with a tablespoon of grated Parmesan on each bowl.

Ingredients:

- 2 medium bulbs of fennel, chopped
- 2 medium stems of leeks, chopped
- 1 to 2 bay leaves
- Salt, to taste (optional)
- 4 cups of vegetable stock
- 1 tablespoon of oil
- ¼ cup of grated Parmesan cheese

Preparation time: 10 minutes
Cooking time: 15 minutes
Serves: 4

SEAFOOD CORN CHOWDER

This is a great seafood chowder that can be on your table in about 20 minutes. Feel free to experiment with your favorite seafood, such a shrimp or other fish. Serve with a green salad and warm bread for an easy weeknight meal.

Directions:

1. Add the oil into the inner pot of the Instant Pot®. Press the sauté key and adjust to normal mode. Once the oil is hot, add the onions, garlic and bell pepper and sauté for 5 minutes or until soft and tender. Add the scallops and fish, cook for 2 minutes and stir in the pepper, tomatoes, vegetable stock, cumin and corn kernels into the inner pot and season with salt and pepper.
2. Briefly stir the ingredients and close the lid securely. Rotate the lid clockwise approximately 30 degrees until the mark on the lid is aligned with the "Close" mark position. Position the steam release handle properly and align the pointed end of the steam release handle pointing to "Sealing", indicating that your Instant Pot® is in the sealed position. Switch to "Soup" button to start the cooking process.
3. When the cooking process is done, use the quick release method by sliding the steam handle to venting position until the pressure is fully released.
4. When the floating valve has dropped, carefully remove the lid. To open the lid, hold and turn it counter clockwise to the open position and lift it to open.
5. Portion the soup into individual serving bowls and serve warm with clams and cilantro on top.

Ingredients:

- 2 halibut fillets (skinless), cut into 1-inch pieces
- 4 fresh sea scallops, quartered
- 1 tablespoon of olive oil
- 1 red onion, diced
- 1 green bell pepper, seeded and diced
- 1 teaspoon of minced garlic
- 4 ripe red tomatoes, core removed, diced
- 3 cups of vegetable stock
- 1 cup drained whole corn kernels
- ½ teaspoon of cumin powder
- ½ teaspoon of crushed black pepper
- 1 cup of canned whole baby clams, drained (for serving)
- 1/4 cup loosely packed fresh cilantro leaves (for serving)

Preparation time: 10 minutes
Cooking time: 20 minutes
Serves: 6

CHICKEN ORZO SOUP

We are huge fans of orzo in our house and this soup is a fun new take on ordinary chicken noodle soup. Don't get me wrong, I'm not knocking chicken noodle soup! It's comfort food at its finest. But the way the orzo absorbs the broth somehow makes it extra special. It might be even better the next day, but of course, that's if there is any left!

Directions:

1. Add the oil into the inner pot of your Instant Pot®. Press the sauté key and adjust to normal mode. Once the oil is hot, add the onions, garlic, celery and carrots into the inner pot and cook until soft and tender. Add the chicken and cook until lightly browned on all sides and pour in the stock. Season to taste with salt and pepper and close the lid securely.
2. Rotate the lid clockwise approximately 30 degrees until the mark on the lid is aligned with the "Close" mark position. Position the steam release handle properly and align the pointed end of the steam release handle pointing to "Sealing", indicating that the Instant Pot® is in the sealed position. Press the soup button to start the cooking process.
3. When the cooking process is done, let the pressure release naturally and wait for 15 minutes before opening the lid, or until the floating valve has dropped. When the floating valve has dropped, carefully remove the lid by holding and turning it counter clockwise to the open position and lift it to open.
4. Remove the chicken from the inner pot and shred into small pieces.
5. Portion the cooked pasta and shredded chicken into individual serving bowls, pour with hot broth and serve warm with chopped green onions and sliced lemons.

Ingredients:

- 1 pound boneless, skinless chicken pieces
- 4-5 cups chicken stock (depending on how broth you like your soup)
- 1 large carrot, peeled and cubed
- 2 medium stalks of celery stalks, chopped
- 1 red onion, diced or quartered
- 1 teaspoon of minced garlic
- 1 cup of orzo pasta, cooked ahead
- ½ to 1 teaspoon of salt
- ½ teaspoon of crushed black pepper
- 1 organic lemon, sliced into wedges
- 2 green onions, chopped

Preparation time: **5 minutes**
Cooking time: **20 minutes**
Serves: **4-6**

FISHERMAN'S SEAFOOD CHOWDER

This is the real deal when it comes to seafood chowders. It is packed full of seafood: shrimp, salmon, lobster... And feel free to add or subtract your favorite seafood to suit your taste buds. It is seasoned just enough so it's got a little zip to it. The best part is you can just throw the ingredients into the pressure cooker and get an A+ dish in under half an hour.

Directions:

1. Add the oil into the inner pot, press the sauté button and add the onions, garlic, celery and tomatoes. Sauté until soft and fragrant and add the seafood ingredients. Cook for about 3 minutes and add the remaining ingredients except for the thickener in the inner pot. Briefly stir to combine and close the lid securely.
2. Rotate the handle clockwise to the lock the lid and position the steam handle to sealing position. Press the soup button and set the cooking time to 10 minutes.
3. When the Instant Pot® has completed the cooking process, let the pressure release naturally until the float valve drops down. Let it stand for 10 minutes to further cook with low heat, open the lid and add the thicken ingredients. Stir to combine and cook until it returns to a boil or until the soup has thickened to desired consistency.
4. Open the lid and transfer to a serving bowl. Serve immediately with lemon wedges, if desired.

Ingredients:

- 1 cup of water
- 2 cups of chicken stock
- 1 tablespoon cooking oil
- 1 medium onion, diced
- 2 red tomatoes, diced
- ½ cup corn kernels
- 1 medium celery stalk, chopped
- 2 teaspoons minced garlic
- ½ cup tomato sauce
- 2 bay leaves
- 1 tablespoon cayenne pepper
- 1 tablespoon paprika
- 1 cup small shrimp, peeled and deveined
- 1 cup canned clams, drained
- 1 cup mussels
- 1 cup squat lobster tails
- 1 cup chopped salmon

Thickener

- 1 tablespoon of flour
- 1 tablespoon of butter
- ½ cup of white wine

Preparation time: 10 minutes
Cooking time: 25 minutes
Serves: 4 to 6

CLAM CHOWDER

This recipe is surprisingly easy for as tasty as this soup is. There is very little prep and very little to clean up. That's my favorite type of recipe! This is great with salad and bread and we love to serve it with oyster crackers.

Directions:

1. Add the chopped bacon into the inner pot of the Instant Pot®. Press the sauté key and adjust to "more" mode to cook the bacon. When the bacon has released most of its fats, adjust to "normal" mode and sauté the onions until tender. Pour in wine and reduce the liquid mixture into half while scraping the bottom of the pot to remove the browned bits. Add the potatoes, clam juice, bay leaf, dried thyme and crushed red pepper flakes and briefly stir the ingredients.
2. Close the lid securely. Rotate the lid clockwise approximately 30 degrees until the mark on the lid is aligned with the "Close" mark position. Position the steam release handle properly and align the pointed end of the steam release handle pointing to "Sealing", indicating that the pressure cooker is in the sealed position. Press the soup button to start the cooking process.
3. While cooking the soup, combine the 2 tablespoons of flour and butter in a small bowl and whisk to combine. Set aside.
4. When the cooking process is done, let the pressure release naturally and wait for 15 minutes before opening the lid, or until the floating valve has dropped. When the floating valve has dropped, carefully remove the lid by holding and turning it counter clockwise to the open position and lift it to open.
5. Stir in the roux, milk, clams and cream into the inner pot. Select the manual function and stir briefly, close the lid and set the cooking time to 5 minutes to return the mixture into a boil.
6. Open lid, adjust seasoning and consistency according to preference. Remove bay leaf. Portion into individual serving bowls, top with parsley or green onions and serve with crackers or garlic croutons.

Preparation time: 5 minutes
Cooking time: 15 minutes
Serves: 4 to 6

Ingredients:

- 1 cup of canned clams, drained
- 2 cups of canned clam juice
- ½ cup of Pancetta or smoked bacon, chopped
- 1 medium white onion, finely chopped
- 1 cup of sake or white wine
- 1 large potato, cut into cubes
- 1 bay leaf
- 1 teaspoon of dried thyme leaves
- 1 to 2 pinches of crushed red peppers or cayenne pepper, for extra heat
- 1 ½ cup of milk
- ½ cup of cream
- 1 tablespoon of unsalted butter, melted
- 2 tablespoons of flour
- Salt and crushed black pepper
- Dried parsley and chopped green onions, for garnish
- Crackers or garlic croutons, for serving

YELLOW SPLIT-PEA SOUP WITH KALE AND POTATOES

This is such a colorful, interesting soup that it is really hard not to fall in love with it. It has the perfect amount of seasoning and even those who are dubious about kale won't be able to complain. Such an easy way to fuel your body with healthy veggies!

Directions:

1. Add the oil into the inner pot of your Instant Pot®. Press the sauté key and adjust to normal mode. Once the oil is hot, add and sauté the onions for 5 minutes or until tender. Transfer the onions on one side of the inner pot, add the mustard and cumin and cook until the seeds are lightly toasted, or until it starts to pop out. Stir in the minced garlic and ginger, cook for about 1 minute and add the potatoes, peas, curry paste and pour in the stock.
2. Season to taste with salt and pepper, stir to combine the ingredients evenly and close the lid. Rotate the lid clockwise approximately 30 degrees until the mark on the lid is aligned with the "Close" mark position. Position the steam release handle properly and align the pointed end of the steam release handle pointing to "Sealing", indicating that the pressure cooker is in the sealed position. Press the soup button to start the cooking process.
3. When the cooking process is done, let the pressure release naturally and wait for 15 minutes before opening the lid, or until the floating valve has dropped. When the floating valve has dropped, carefully remove the lid by holding and turning it counter clockwise to the open position and lift it to open. Add the chopped kale and stir to distribute the ingredients evenly. Set to keep warm mode, close the lid and let it cook for 10 minutes before serving.
4. Portion the soup into individual serving bowls, serve warm with chopped fresh parsley if desired.

Ingredients:

- 1 large red onion, minced
- ½ tablespoon of cumin seeds
- ½ tablespoon of black mustard seeds
- 1 tablespoon of canola oil
- 1 1-inch piece of fresh ginger root, minced
- 2 to 3 garlic cloves, minced
- 2 cups of diced sweet potatoes
- 8 cups of vegetable stock or water
- ½ pound of yellow split peas, rinsed and drained
- 2 to 3 tablespoons of curry paste
- Salt and pepper, as needed to taste
- 1 cup of chopped kale
- Chopped parsley for garnish (optional)

Preparation time: 10 minutes
Cooking time: 20 minutes
Serves: 8

BLACK BEAN SOUP WITH AVOCADO SALSA

The avocado salsa is really the star of the show in this soup. It just adds something extra special to what is already a delicious dish. Adjust the spiciness of the salsa by adding more or less jalapeño according to your preference.

Directions:

1. Prepare the avocado salsa by adding all ingredients into a large bowl, gently toss the ingredients to combine evenly.
2. Add the oil into the inner pot of the pressure cooker. Press the sauté key and adjust to normal mode. Once the oil is hot, add the onions, cumin seeds, chili powder and dried oregano and cook for 5 minutes, or until the onions are tender. Stir in the garlic, black beans, chorizo, bay leaves and pour in the stock. Season to taste with salt and white pepper and close the lid securely.
3. Rotate the lid clockwise approximately 30 degrees until the mark on the lid is aligned with the "Close" mark position. Position the steam release handle properly and align the pointed end of the steam release handle pointing to "Sealing", indicating that the Instant Pot® is in the sealed position. Press the soup button to start the cooking process.
4. When the cooking process is done, let the pressure release naturally and wait for 15 minutes before opening the lid, or until the floating valve has dropped. When the floating valve has dropped, carefully remove the lid by holding and turning it counter clockwise to the open position and lift it to open. Remove the bay leaf, discard it and adjust consistency by adding more stock or water until the desired consistency is achieved.
5. Portion the soup into individual serving bowls and serve warm with a dollop of avocado salsa.

Preparation time: 15 minutes
Cooking time: 20 minutes
Serves: 8

Ingredients:

For the Soup

- 2 to 3 teaspoons of oil
- 1 medium white onion, diced
- 2 to 3 teaspoons of crushed chili pepper flakes or hot chili powder
- ½ tablespoon of toasted cumin seeds
- ½ tablespoon of dried oregano leaves
- 7 to 8 cups of vegetable stock or water
- 2 to 2 1/2 cups of canned black beans, drained
- 3 links of Spanish chorizo, casings removed and chopped
- 2 to 3 teaspoons of minced garlic
- 2 bay leaves
- Salt and ground white pepper, to taste

For the Avocado Salsa

- 1 large ripe any variety of avocado, pitted, thinly sliced or diced
- 2 ripe red tomatoes, seeded and diced
- 1 small red onion, halved and thinly sliced
- ¼ cup of loosely packed fresh cilantro leaves, chopped
- 1 green chili or jalapeño, sliced
- 2 limes, juiced
- Salt, as needed to adjust taste

TURKEY, SWEET POTATO AND BLACK BEAN CHILI

This is a fall and winter staple at our house. It's healthy, easy and so darn good! The kids gobble it up and I feel good because it full of sweet potatoes, tomatoes and other things that are full of nutrients. The spices can be adjusted to your preference. This version is fairly mild, but by increasing the cayenne you can certainly ramp up the heat. This is definitely one of my favorites.

Directions:

1. Press the sauté button and allow the inner pot to begin to warm. Add ground turkey and onion and cook until turkey is browned and onion is soft. Add the garlic and cook for two more minutes.
2. Add the rest of the ingredients to the inner pot and stir until well incorporated.
3. Close the lid securely. Rotate the lid clockwise approximately 30 degrees until the mark on the lid is aligned with the "Close" mark position. Position the steam release handle properly and align the pointed end of the steam release handle pointing to "Sealing", indicating that the Instant Pot® is in the sealed position. Press the soup button to start the cooking process.
4. When the cooking process is complete, allow pressure to release naturally. When the float valve drops, open the lid carefully. Stir and adjust seasonings. Add more cayenne to make chili spicier.
5. Ladle into bowls and serve.

Ingredients:

- 1 pound ground turkey
- 1 small onion, chopped
- 1 tbsp minced garlic
- 2-3 small sweet potatoes, peeled and cubed into bite size chunks
- 1 can black beans (15 oz)
- 1 can fire roasted tomatoes with juice (14.5 oz)
- 1 bay leaf
- 1 tsp cumin
- 1/2 tsp oregano
- 1/8 tsp salt
- 1/2 tsp ground pepper
- 1/4 tsp cayenne pepper
- 1 1/2 cups water

Preparation time: 10 minutes
Cooking time: 40 minutes
Serves: 6

PORK AND HOMINY STEW

This is a simple stew that is full of flavor and has just enough heat that you'll want to keep a drink handy! The Instant Pot® gets the pork nice and tender.

Ingredients:

- 1 pound of lean pork meat, cut into 2-inch cubes
- Salt and crushed black pepper
- 2 teaspoons of cooking oil
- ½ large sweet onion, diced
- 2 teaspoons of minced garlic
- 2 tablespoons of crushed crushed red pepper flakes, or more as needed for extra heat
- 4 to 5 cups of chicken stock
- 1 cup of vegetable stock or water
- 2 cups of canned hominy, rinsed and drained
- 1 medium ripe avocado, halved, pitted and thinly sliced
- 2 limes, sliced into wedges, for serving
- Chopped fresh cilantro leaves, for garnish

Preparation time: 5 minutes
Cooking time: 20 minutes
Serves: 6

Directions:

1. Place the pork in a large bowl, season with generous amounts of salt and pepper. Add 1 teaspoon of oil into the inner pot of the pressure cooker. Press the sauté key and adjust to "more" mode to brown the meat. When the oil is hot, add half of the meat and brown evenly on all sides. Remove from your Instant Pot®, transfer onto a plate and set aside. Add the remaining meat and cook until browned evenly on all sides. Remove meat from the inner pot and place it on the plate.

2. Add the remaining oil into the inner pot, add the onions, garlic and chili flakes and cook for about 3 minutes until soft and aromatic. Pour the stock and water into the inner pot, stir with a wooden spoon and scrape the bottom of the pot to remove the browned bits. Return the meat into the pressure cooker and close the lid securely.

3. Rotate the lid clockwise approximately 30 degrees until the mark on the lid is aligned with the "Close" mark position. Position the steam release handle properly and align the pointed end of the steam release handle pointing to "Sealing", indicating that the pressure cooker is in the sealed position. Select the stew function to start the cooking process.

4. When the cooking process is done, use the quick release method by sliding the steam handle to venting position until the pressure is fully released.

5. Skim off oil and bubbles that floats on the top surface of the inner pot and remove the meat with a slotted spoon. Place into a cutting board or bowl, shred the meat with two forks and return into the inner pot together with the hominy.

6. Close the lid and wait for 15 minutes, or until the hominy is warmed through before serving. Adjust seasoning and consistency of soup until the desired taste and thickness is achieved.

7. Portion the soup into individual serving bowls, serve warm with avocado and lime slices and chopped cilantro on top.

CREAMY POTATO SOUP

My kids and I love a good potato soup. There is something about it that is hard to beat on a cold day. We like to load it up with extra cheddar and bacon bits. Serve it with a tossed salad and warm bread for a quick meal after playing in the cold!

Directions:

1. Add onions, potatoes, celery and the stock into the inner pot of the pressure cooker. Season to taste with salt and pepper, and then briefly stir to combine.
2. Close the lid securely. Rotate the lid clockwise approximately 30 degrees until the mark on the lid is aligned with the "Close" mark position. Position the steam release handle properly and align the pointed end of the steam release handle pointing to "Sealing", indicating that the Instant Pot® is in the sealed position. Press the soup button to start the cooking process.
3. When the cooking process is done, let the pressure release naturally and wait for 15 minutes before opening the lid, or until the floating valve has dropped. When the floating valve has dropped, carefully remove the lid by holding and turning it counter clockwise to the open position and lift it to open.
4. Stir in the butter, cream and milk, season to taste with salt and white pepper. Briefly stir the ingredients and close the lid. Wait for 10 to 15 minutes before serving, or until the butter has melted.
5. Portion the soup into individual serving bowls, serve warm with grated cheddar cheese on top.

Ingredients:

- 1 ½ pounds of potatoes, peeled and cut into small cubes
- 6 medium celery stalks, roughly chopped
- 1 cup of diced white onion
- 5 to 6 cups of vegetable or chicken stock
- 1 ½ cups of milk
- ½ cup of cream
- ¼ cup of unsalted butter
- Salt and ground white pepper, to taste
- ¼ cup of grated cheddar cheese, for serving

Preparation time: **10 minutes**
Cooking time: **20 minutes**
Serves: **8**

EASY BEEF STEW

I love the rustic, hearty flavors that this stew develops as the Instant Pot® works its magic. It's perfect for a cool fall evening or a cold snowy night. Serve with cornbread, biscuits, or whatever makes your family happy!

Directions:

1. Mix the flour, pepper, salt and steak seasoning in a large bowl and mix until well combined. Add the beef and toss to coat it evenly with the flour mixture.
2. Add the oil in the inner pot, press the sauté button and adjust to brown mode. Add half of the beef and brown evenly on all sides. Remove and transfer to a plate. Brown the remaining beef until all sides are evenly browned and add it into to first batch of browned beef. Set aside.
3. Add the onions and sauté until soft and translucent. Pour in the stock, Worcestershire sauce and add the stock cube. Stir until all solid ingredients are completely dissolved.
4. Put browned meat back into the pot. Add the carrots, potatoes, celery and bay leaves into the inner pot. Close the lid, rotate the handle to lock the pressure cooker and position the steam vent handle to sealing position Press the meat/stew button and adjust to more/high mode and cook until the pressure cooker switches to keep warm mode. Let the pressure release naturally until the float valve drops down. Let it stand for 10 minutes before opening lid to finish the cooking process with low heat.
5. Open the lid and remove the meat and vegetables from the inner pot. Portion the meat and vegetables into individual serving bowls, set aside. Cook the sauce further until the desired consistency is achieved and adjust seasoning if needed. Pour the sauce into the serving bowls and serve immediately.

Ingredients:

- 2 pounds of beef meat, for stewing
- 5 to 6 tablespoons of all-purpose flour
- 1 tablespoon of steak seasoning
- ½ teaspoon of ground black pepper
- ½ teaspoon of salt
- 2 tablespoons of cooking oil
- 1 white onion, chopped
- 2 bay leaves
- 4 tablespoons of Worcestershire sauce
- 3 cups brown beef stock
- 1 beef stock cube
- 1 pound of red potatoes, peeled and cubed
- 1 pound of carrots, peeled, sliced into 1/2 –inch rounds
- 1 medium stalk of celery, chopped

Preparation time: **15 minutes**
Cooking time: **45 minutes**
Serves: **8**

CHICKEN NOODLE SOUP

There is nothing like chicken noodle soup, especially when you are sick. It's packed with healthy nutrients, it's easy to eat and it is just comfortable. Here is an easy soup that uses leftover chicken to create a meal that will warm and soothe you.

Directions:

1. Add oil into the inner pot and press sauté button. When oil is hot, add carrots, onion and celery and sauté for about 3-4 minutes until vegetables are slightly soft and aromatic.
2. Add all remaining ingredients to the inner pot, briefly stir to combine and close the lid.
3. Lock the lid and position the steam release handle to sealing position. Press the soup button and set the cooking time to 7 minutes.
4. When the Instant Pot® has completed the cooking cycle, use the quick release method to release the pressure fully until the float valve drops down. Open the lid and season to taste with salt and black pepper.
5. Portion the noodles into individual serving bowls and ladle in the warm soup. Serve warm with chopped green onions on top.

Ingredients:

- 1 tablespoon oil
- 7 cups of chicken stock
- ½ pound of pasta or egg noodles
- 2 cups of shredded/chopped cooked chicken
- 1 cup finely diced carrots
- 1 small onion, diced
- 1/2 cup finely chopped celery
- 1 tablespoon of chicken bouillon base
- 1 tablespoon dry white wine
- Salt and black pepper, to taste
- 2 stems of green onions, chopped for serving

Preparation time: 5 minutes
Cooking time: 15 minutes
Serves: 4

Pork

PEPPERED SWEET PORK RIBS

This sauce in this dish is incredible and will have you wanting to lick your plate. It's a touch spicy, a touch peppery and will leave you wanting more the next day. Because of the slow cook time at the end, it takes a bit longer to make than traditional pressure cooker recipes, but the end results are worth it. These ribs are fall off the bone good!

Directions:

1. Combine together all sauce ingredients and mix until all ingredients are evenly distributed. Set aside.
2. Add the oil into the inner pot of the pressure cooker. Press the sauté key and adjust to more mode to sear the pork ribs. When the oil is hot, brown half of the ribs until all sides are seared evenly. Remove from the inner pot and brown the remaining ribs. Return the browned ribs together with the water and the sauce mixture. Mix the ingredients to coat the ribs evenly with the sauce. Close the lid securely and rotate the lid clockwise approximately 30 degrees until the mark on the lid is aligned with the "Close" mark position. Position the steam release handle properly and align the pointed end of the steam release handle to "Sealing", indicating that the pressure cooker is in the sealed position. Press the meat/stew button and to start cooking ribs with high temperature.
3. When the cooking process is done, let the pressure release naturally and wait for 15 minutes, or until the floating valve has dropped.
4. When the floating valve has dropped, carefully remove the lid by holding and turning it counter clockwise to the open position and lift it to open. Turn the meat to coat evenly with sauce, close the lid.
5. Switch the Instant Pot® into slow cook mode, set the cooking time to 1 hour and adjust to "less" mode (low).

Ingredients:

- 1 medium rack of pork short ribs (or about 2 pounds), chopped into portions with 2 rib bones each
- 2 teaspoons of sesame oil
- ¼ cup of stock or water

For the sauce
- 3 to 4 tablespoons of light soy sauce
- 2 tablespoons of raw cane sugar
- 2 tablespoons of honey
- ½ tablespoon of minced garlic
- ½ cup barbecue sauce or ketchup
- 1 medium red onion, minced
- 1 tablespoon of dark molasses (substitute maple syrup in a pinch)
- 2 to 3 tablespoons of cider vinegar
- ½ to 1 tablespoon of hot chili sauce or Sriracha sauce
- 1 pinch of salt
- 1 teaspoon of crushed black pepper

Preparation time: 10 minutes
Cooking time: 1 hour 30 minutes
Serves: 4 to 6

6. After the slow cook cooking time, open the lid and transfer the ribs onto a serving dish. Pour the sauce over ribs and serve warm.

PORK CHOPS WITH CABBAGE

If you like simple recipes with very little prep, then this is the recipe for you. The fennel adds great flavor to the dish and the gravy is delicious. Even my husband, who was unsure about the cabbage, enjoyed this dish.

Directions:

1. Pat meat dry with paper towels, and season with fennel seeds, salt and pepper.
2. Add 1 tablespoon of oil into the inner pot of the pressure cooker. Press the sauté key and adjust to "more/brown" mode. Once the oil is hot, brown the meat in separate batches evenly on all sides. Remove the first batch from the inner pot and brown the remaining pork chops. Remove the pork chops, transfer on a plate and set aside.
3. Place the cabbage into the inner pot, add the browned pork chops over the cabbage leaves and arrange them well for even cooking. Pour the stock into the inner pot and close the lid securely.
4. Rotate the lid clockwise approximately 30 degrees until the mark on the lid is aligned with the "Close" mark position. Position the steam release handle properly and align the pointed end of the steam release handle pointing to "Sealing", indicating that the pressure cooker is in the sealed position. Press the meat/stew button to start the cooking process.
5. When your Instant Pot® reaches pressure, press the "keep-warm/cancel" button and reset to slow cook mode. Set the cooking time to 30 minutes and adjust to "normal" mode.
6. When the cooking process is done, let the pressure release naturally and wait for 15 minutes before opening the lid, or until the floating valve has dropped. Carefully remove the lid by holding and turning it counter clockwise to the open position and lift it to open. Adjust seasoning according to preferred taste.
7. Portion the cabbage leaves on individual serving bowls, top with pork chops and serve immediately.

Ingredients:

- 4 2cm-thick pork chops
- ½ tablespoon of crushed fennel seeds
- ½ teaspoon of salt
- 1 teaspoon of crushed black peppercorns
- 1 pound or small head of cabbage, core removed, cut into half and sliced into 1-inch thick
- 1 tablespoon of cooking oil
- 1 cup of vegetable stock
- 1 tablespoon of flour

Preparation time: 8 minutes
Cooking time: 1 hour
Serves: 4

PULLED PORK

Pulled pork in under an hour? Yes, please! This is such an enjoyable dish that will please the whole family and is great for those nights when you just don't know what to make for dinner.

Directions:

1. Combine all ingredients for the dry rub in a bowl and mix until well incorporated. Add the meat and rub the mixture evenly on all sides. Add the oil into the inner pot of the pressure cooker. Press the sauté key and adjust to more mode to sear the meat. Once the oil is hot, brown the meat evenly on all sides. You may brown the meat separately to avoid overcrowding and to have a nice sear on the meat. Return all portions of the meat into the inner pot, pour in the water and beer and close the lid securely.
2. Rotate the lid clockwise approximately 30 degrees until the mark on the lid is aligned with the "Close" mark position. Position the steam release handle properly and align the pointed end of the steam release handle pointing to "Sealing", indicating that the pressure cooker is in the sealed position. Press the "meat/stew" button and adjust cooking time to 20 minutes. The pressure cooker allows adjusting the cooking time within the first 10 seconds after pressing meat/stew button.
3. While cooking the meat, mix sugar and hot water in a bowl and mix until the sugar is completely dissolved. Add the remaining sauce ingredients and mix until well incorporated. Set aside.
4. When the cooking process is done, use the quick release method by sliding the steam handle to venting position until the pressure is fully released.
5. When the floating valve has dropped, carefully remove the lid. To open the lid, hold and turn it counter clockwise to the open position and lift it to open. Remove the meat, transfer to a bowl and shred meat with two forks.
6. Return the shredded meat into the inner pot with the cooking liquid and add the sauce mixture from step 3. Toss to coat the meat evenly with the sauce and press the sauté button. Adjust to more mode and cook for about 5 minutes or until the sauce has thickened and the meat is evenly coated with the sauce. Switch to keep warm mode and transfer the meat to a serving dish. Serve warm with extra barbecue sauce.

Preparation time: 10 minutes
Cooking time: 40 minutes
Serves: 6 to 8

Ingredients:

For the pulled pork
- 6 pounds of pork shoulder, cut into two portions
- 1 cup of beer
- 1 tablespoon of oil
- 1 cup of water

For the Dry Rub
- 6 tablespoons of sugar
- ½ tablespoon of paprika
- ½ tablespoon of dry mustard
- ½ tablespoon of salt

For the Sauce
- 1 ½ cup of apple cider vinegar
- 2 tablespoons of raw cane sugar
- ½ cup of hot water
- ½ tablespoon of ground black pepper
- ¼ to ½ tablespoon of salt
- 1 to 2 teaspoons of cayenne pepper
- ½ tablespoon of dry mustard

JAPANESE PORK BELLY

Do you have someone you'd like to impress? Then this is your dish! Normally Japanese pork belly can take hours of your time, adjusting temperatures and making sure you have the right amount of liquid. Using the Instant Pot® makes this dish much more accessible. Serve in a bowl over rice.

Directions:

1. Place the pork belly in a bowl, add the 7-spice mix and crushed peppercorns and rub evenly on all areas of the meat.
2. Add the oil into the inner pot of your Instant Pot®. Press the sauté key and adjust to "more/brown" mode. Once the oil is hot, brown the pork belly portions on all sides. This can be done in batches if needed. Pour in enough stock to cover the meat. Add the ginger and scallions, stir to distribute the ingredients evenly and close the lid securely.
3. Rotate the lid clockwise approximately 30 degrees until the mark on the lid is aligned with the "Close" mark position. Position the steam release handle properly and align the pointed end of the steam release handle pointing to "Sealing", indicating that the pressure cooker is in the sealed position. Press the meat/stew button to start the cooking process.
4. When the cooking process is done, let the pressure release naturally and wait for 15 minutes before opening the lid, or until the floating valve has dropped. Leave the pork belly in the pressure cooker for 30 minutes to cook slowly with low heat. Carefully remove the lid by holding and turning it counter clockwise to the open position and lift it to open.
5. Remove the pork belly with a slotted spoon, drain the cooking liquid and discard with the vegetables. Add the flavoring ingredients into the inner pot and mix until the sugar is completely dissolved. Return the pork belly into the inner pot together with the eggs, close the lid securely. Press the sauté button and adjust to "more" mode, bring to a boil and cook for about 5 minutes with open lid or until the alcohol from the sake has been released.
6. Press the "keep warm/cancel" button, close and position lid to close mark with the steam release in sealing position. Press the slow cook button, set the timer to 1 hour and adjust to "less" mode by pressing the minus button repeatedly.
7. When the slow cooking process is done, let the pressure release naturally and wait for 15 minutes before opening the lid, or until the floating valve has dropped. Carefully remove the lid by holding and turning it counter clockwise to the open position and lift it to open. For a thicker sauce consistency, press the sauté button and adjust to normal mode to cook with open lid. Press the "keep-warm/cancel" button when the desired thickness is achieved.
8. Portion the soup, eggs and meat into individual serving bowls, serve warm with extra flavoring sauce.

Preparation time: 10 minutes
Cooking time: 1 hour to 1 hour 30 minutes
Serves: 4

Ingredients:

- 3 medium scallions, white parts removed, green parts chopped
- 1-inch piece of fresh ginger root, slice into thin rounds
- 1 tablespoon of olive or cooking oil
- 1 piece of pork belly (or about 2 pounds), cut into 4 portions
- 1 cup of vegetable stock
- 4 hard-boiled medium whole eggs, shells removed
- 2 tablespoons of Japanese 7-spice mix
- 1 teaspoon of crushed black peppercorns

Other Flavoring Ingredients

- 6 tablespoons of sake
- ½ cup of stock
- 2 tablespoons of tamari soy sauce
- 3 tablespoons of light soy sauce
- 3 to 4 tablespoons of brown sugar

PORK WITH TOMATOES

Don't let the long ingredient list scare you from making this tasty dish. Most of the list consists of spices that are probably in your cabinet. They add so much flavor to the pork.

Directions:

1. Pat meat dry with paper towels, place in a bowl and season with salt and pepper.
2. Add 1 tablespoon of oil into the inner pot of the pressure cooker. Press the sauté key and adjust to "more/brown" mode. Once the oil is hot, brown half of the meat cubes evenly on all sides and remove from the inner pot. Brown the remaining meat on all sides and place it in a bowl, set aside.
3. Heat the remaining oil in the inner pot, add the onions and a pinch of salt and sauté until tender. Add the minced garlic, smoked paprika, mustard seeds, cayenne, cumin and crushed cloves and cook for 5 minutes or until aromatic. Slowly add the flour while stirring occasionally, cook until lightly brown and add the tomatoes, sugar, browned meat, wine vinegar and the stock. Cook for 5 minutes while stirring and scraping the bottom of the pot to remove the browned bits.
4. Close the lid and rotate it clockwise approximately 30 degrees until the mark on the lid is aligned with the "Close" mark position. Position the steam release handle properly and align the pointed end of the steam release handle pointing to "Sealing", indicating that your Instant Pot® is in the sealed position. Press the meat/stew button to start the cooking process. Set time for 45 minutes.
5. When the cooking process is done, let the pressure release naturally and wait for 15 minutes before opening the lid, or until the floating valve has dropped. Leave it for about 30 minutes in the pressure cooker to cook slowly with low heat. Carefully remove the lid by holding and turning it counter clockwise to the open position and lift it to open.
6. Portion it into individual serving bowls, and serve warm with minced cilantro.

Preparation time: 10 minutes
Cooking time: 1 hour, 30 minutes
Serves: 6

Ingredients:

- 2 ½ to 3 pounds of pork butt roast, bone removed and trimmed, cut into 1-inch cubes
- Salt and ground pepper
- 2 tablespoons cooking oil
- 2 large red onions, minced
- 2 tablespoons of minced garlic
- 2 teaspoons of mustard seeds, crushed
- 2 teaspoons of smoked paprika
- ½ tablespoon of cumin powder
- 2 pinches of cayenne pepper
- 2 whole cloves, crushed
- 3 tablespoons of flour
- 1 cup chicken stock
- 2 cups of canned tomatoes, diced
- 3 tablespoons of red wine vinegar
- 1 tablespoon of sugar
- ¼ cup of loosely packed fresh cilantro leaves, minced

HONEY-GARLIC PORK RIBS

Yum! The sauce in this dish is amazing and the pork is so tender. This one is a favorite in our dinner rotation and any time we have it the kids go back for seconds… and thirds! This is definitely a recipe to try soon.

Directions:

1. Combine all ingredients for the marinade in a bowl and whisk until well incorporated. Place the meat on a covered container, pour the marinade mixture over the meat and coat the meat evenly with sauce. Chill for at least 2 hours to marinate the meat and to allow the flavors to penetrate into the meat. Remove the meat from the marinade mixture and drain, reserving the marinade.
2. Add 1 tablespoon of oil into the inner pot of the pressure cooker. Press the sauté key and adjust to "normal" mode. Cook the meat until the meat starts to brown while turning occasionally. Pour the marinade mixture and toss to evenly coat the meat.
3. Close the lid securely. Rotate the lid clockwise approximately 30 degrees until the mark on the lid is aligned with the "Close" mark position. Position the steam release handle to "venting" mode. Press the slow cook button, set the cooking time for 2 hours and adjust to normal "mode/medium heat".
4. When the cooking process is done, leave it for 30 minutes to continue cooking with low heat. Carefully remove the lid by holding and turning it counter clockwise to the open position and lift it to open. Stir the meat and sauce mixture to evenly coat the meat.
5. Transfer into a serving platter and serve immediately.

Ingredients:

- 2 pounds of pork ribs (spareribs or back ribs), cut into 1-rib portions
- 1 tablespoon of oil

For the marinade

- ½ cup of honey
- 1 tablespoon of lemon juice
- ½ cup loosely packed raw cane sugar
- 3 tablespoons of tamari soy sauce
- 1 teaspoon of garlic powder
- 1 teaspoon of ginger powder
- 1 teaspoon of yellow mustard powder

Preparation time: 10 minutes
Cooking time: 2 hours and 30 minutes
Serves: 4

PORK SHOULDER

A pork shoulder can be a little intimidating if you've never prepared one before. It's a big chunk of meat and I was always afraid I'd cook it wrong and ruin the whole piece. Luckily, the Instant Pot® takes most of the guess work out of the preparation. This is a very beginner friendly recipe that yields great results. Serve the shredded meat with barbecue sauce on a sandwich or use in other dishes.

Directions:

1. Add 1 tablespoon of oil into the inner pot of the pressure cooker. Press the sauté key and adjust to "more/brown" mode. Sear all sides of the meat until lightly browned, add the ham base, pepper and the stock.
2. Close the lid securely. Rotate the lid clockwise approximately 30 degrees until the mark on the lid is aligned with the "Close" mark position. Position the steam release handle to "sealing" mode. Press the "meat/stew" button and adjust to normal "mode/medium heat" mode. Let it cook for one hour.
3. When the cooking process is done, leave it for 30 minutes to continue cooking with low heat. Carefully remove the lid by holding and turning it counter clockwise to the open position and lift it to open. Remove the meat from the inner pot with a tong, transfer into a large plate and let it rest to cool. Shred the meat with two forks, remove and discard connective tissues and excess fats.
4. Chill or immediately use with other recipes.

Ingredients:

- 3 pounds of pork shoulder/butt, bone removed and excess fat trimmed, divided into 3 portions
- 2 cups of beef stock
- 3 tablespoons of ham base bouillon
- 1 teaspoon of pepper

Preparation time: 20 minutes
Cooking time: 1 hour 30 minutes
Serves: 6

PORK LOIN

This is an easy, fool proof way to serve a delicious pork roast with gravy. Growing up, pork roast was something that we usually had on a Sunday, but the pressure cooker makes this so convenient that you can have pork roast any night of the week.

Directions:

1. Season meat with Italian seasoning and minced garlic, rub evenly on all areas.
2. Add the oil into the inner pot of the pressure cooker. Press the sauté button and adjust to "more/brown" mode. Add half of the onions and sauté until soft and translucent. Add the meat and brown on all areas, remove from the inner pot and place it on a plate.
3. Pour in 3 cups of stock, add a trivet in the pot and place the meat over it. Add the remaining onions, close the lid and lock it in the pressure cooker. Position the steam vent handle to sealing position and press the meat/stew button. Set the cooking time to 1 hour and adjust to "normal/medium heat" mode.
4. When the Instant Pot® has switched to keep warm mode, let the pressure release naturally. Remove the meat, transfer to a plate and tent with foil to keep it warm.
5. Remove the trivet from the inner pot, add the remaining stock, salt, pepper and water-cornstarch mixture and stir to combine. Reset the pressure to "sauté" mode and adjust to more/brown" mode. Bring to a boil while stirring regularly, press the "keep warm/cancel" button to stop cooking.
6. Serve the pork roast warm with gravy on the side.

Ingredients:

- 3 pounds of bone-in pork loin
- 6 cups of chicken stock
- 3 tablespoons of oil
- 3 minced garlic cloves
- 1 medium red onion, core removed and quartered
- 3 tablespoons of Italian seasoning
- ¼ cup mixture of equal amounts of water and cornstarch
- 1 teaspoon of ground black pepper
- 1 teaspoon of salt

Preparation time: 15 minutes
Cooking time: 1 hour
Serves: 6

PORK TENDERLOIN

Every time I prepare this dish I wonder why I don't make it more often. It's simple, delicious and everyone loves it. Don't skip marinating the meat. It adds so much extra flavor, you'll be glad you did it!

Directions:

1. Place the cilantro, garlic, crushed red pepper flakes, salt, lime juice and oil in a food processor or blender. Pulse until a smooth consistency is achieved. Transfer the mixture into a resealable plastic bag and the trimmed tenderloin. Squeeze out the air inside the bag to coat the meat completely. Chill for at least 4 hours to marinate the meat.
2. Place the stock and lemon juice in the inner pot, add the meat and marinade mixture and stir just to combine. Close the lid securely, rotate clockwise to lock the pressure cooker and position the steam vent handle to sealing position. Press the "meat/stew" button to start cooking.
3. When the Instant Pot® switches to keep warm mode, release the pressure naturally until floating valve drops. Leave it for another 10 minutes before opening the lid.
4. Remove the meat with tongs or a slotted spoon and slice it into 2-inch thick pieces. Place the meat slices on a serving platter or portion into individual serving plates. Serve warm with cooking sauce over meat slices.

Ingredients:

- 3 tablespoons of fresh cilantro leaves
- 3 tablespoons of oil
- 3 tablespoons of fresh lime juice
- 1 teaspoon of minced garlic
- 2 small pinches of crushed red pepper flakes
- 2 small pinches of salt, or to taste
- 1 ½ pounds of pork tenderloin, trimmed and silver-skin removed
- 1 cup of chicken stock
- 2 lemons, juiced and zested

Preparation time: 15 minutes
Cooking time: 25 minutes
Serves: 6

PORK ROAST

This is another easy pork roast recipe, but this one is a one pot meal. One pot meals are always high on my list because they are so simple and there is less mess to clean up after the meal. Carrots and potatoes cook on top of the meat. To add some great flavor to your veggies, serve with the broth that the meat was cooked in.

Directions:

1. Season meat with, salt, crushed peppercorns and everyday seasoning mix and rub evenly on all areas. Place the oil in the inner pot, press the sauté button and adjust to normal mode. When oil is hot, brown the meat on all sides and pour in the stock. Close the lid and rotate to lock the pressure cooker. Position the steam vent handle to sealing position, press the "meat/stew" button and adjust to "more/high heat" mode.
2. When the pressure cooker switches to keep warm mode, let the pressure release naturally until the floater valve drops. Open the lid and add the carrots and potatoes, reset your Instant Pot® to "meat/stew" mode and set the cooking time to 15 minutes.
3. Let it stand for about 10 minutes to make sure the vegetables are tender and cooked through. Remove from the inner pot, transfer into a serving dish and serve immediately.

Ingredients:

- 1 pork roast (about 21/2 or 3 pounds)
- Salt and crushed peppercorns
- 1 tablespoon of oil
- 1 tablespoon of homemade or packaged Everyday Seasoning mix
- 1 ½ cups of beef stock
- 1 pound of baby carrots
- 4 cups of cubed potatoes

Preparation time: 15 minutes
Cooking time: 1 hour 15 minutes
Serves: 4 to 6

CREAMY TENDER PORK CHOPS

This is a crowd pleaser and is a delicious meal to serve to guests. Depending on your time, a nice addition is some onion and fresh mushrooms sautéed after the pork. They can stay in the pot while the Instant Pot® does its work and be scooped out at the end with the sauce.

Directions:

1. Add the oil into the inner pot, press the sauté button and adjust to "brown" mode. Heat the oil until smoking, add the pork chops and brown evenly on both sides. Brown the pork chops in separate batches to have a nice sear, if desired. Remove the meat and transfer to a plate.
2. Pour in the stock and add the chicken bouillon in the inner pot, stir and scrape the bottom to remove the browned bits. Press the sauté button and bring the mixture to a boil. Return the browned pork chops, close the lid and rotate the handle to lock the pressure cooker. Position the steam vent handle to sealing position, reset and press the meat/stew button. Let it cook until it has switched to keep warm mode and let the pressure release naturally. When the floater valve drops, open the lid and remove the pork chops. You may thicken the soup by cooking further until the desired consistency is achieved. Place the pork chops on a dish and cover with foil to keep it warm.
3. Stir in the mushroom soup, sour cream and parsley into the cooking liquid in the inner pot. Cook until heated through by pressing the sauté button and set the cooking time for about 5 minutes.
4. Portion the pork chops into individual serving bowls or dishes and serve immediately with the warm sauce.

Ingredients:

- 6 2 cm-thick pork chops
- Ground black pepper, to taste
- 2 tablespoons of cooking oil
- 1 ½ cups water
- 1 tablespoon chicken bouillon
- 1 cup of canned cream of mushroom soup
- 1 ½ cups sour cream
- 1 sprig of fresh parsley leaves, minced

Preparation time: 10 minutes
Cooking time: 20 minutes
Serves: 4 to 6

VEGETABLES AND PORK CHOPS

This one is another one-pot wonder. This recipe boasts a slight Asian flavor because of the soy and the Worcestershire, but it's just enough to add a little interest.

Directions:

1. Season meat with salt and crushed black peppers and rub evenly on all areas.
2. Add 1 ½ tablespoons of butter into the inner pot, press the sauté button and adjust to brown mode. When butter is melted, add the pork chops and brown evenly all sides. Remove from the inner pot and transfer to a plate.
3. Add the remaining butter into the pot, sauté the onions and carrots until soft and tender. Stir in the Worcestershire sauce, soy sauce and stock, and then return the pork chops into the inner pot. Season to taste with salt and pepper, place the steam rack over the pork chops and place the potatoes in the rack.
4. Close the lid securely and rotate the handle to lock the Instant Pot®. Position the steam vent handle to venting position, press the meat/stew button and cook until the pressure cooker switches to keep warm mode. Let the pressure release naturally until the floating valve drops down and then carefully open the lid. Remove the potatoes and slice into large dices or quarters, remove the pork chops and place them individual serving bowls.
5. Portion the potatoes into individual serving bowls with the pork chops, and then pour over with warm cooking sauce.

Ingredients:

- 4 slices of 1-inch thick pork chops
- Salt and crushed black pepper, as needed to taste
- 3 tablespoons of butter
- ½ pound of baby carrots
- 1 white onion, diced
- 1 cup of vegetable stock
- 1 tablespoons of tamari soy sauce
- 2 tablespoons of Worcestershire sauce
- 1 pound of Russet potatoes

Preparation time: 15 minutes
Cooking time: 25 minutes
Serves: 4

PORK CHOP WITH SAUERKRAUT

I'm going to let you in on a secret… I am not a fan of sauerkraut. But certain members of my family love it and so to be a good sport I will prepare this dish. They are always thrilled and I can enjoy the pork chops and potatoes. I love a meal where everyone is happy!

Directions:

1. Season pork chops with salt and pepper and rub evenly on both sides. Add the oil in the inner pot, press the sauté button and adjust to brown mode. Add half of the meat and brown evenly on both sides, remove from the inner pot and brown the remaining pork chops. Place onto a plate and set aside.
2. Add the sauerkraut in the inner pot, sprinkle with sugar and place the browned pork chops over the fermented cabbage. Add the potatoes and the stock and then season to taste with salt and pepper.
3. Close the lid and rotate the handle to lock the Instant Pot® and position the steam vent to sealing position. Press the meat/stew button and cook until the pressure cooker switches to keep warm mode. Release the pressure naturally until the floater valve drops down. Let it stand for 10 minutes before opening the lid.
4. Remove the potatoes and pork chops from the inner pot. Portion sauerkraut into individual serving dish or bowls and place the potatoes and the pork chops over the cabbage. Pour the cooking sauce over the meat and potatoes and serve immediately.

Ingredients:

- 6 slices of 1-inch thick bone-in pork loin chops
- 2 tablespoons of cooking oil
- 1/2 teaspoon of table salt
- ½ teaspoon crushed black pepper
- 3 cups of sauerkraut (fermented cabbage), drained
- 2 tablespoons of raw cane sugar
- 1 pound peeled potatoes
- 2 cups of vegetable stock

Preparation time: 10 minutes
Cooking time: 25 minutes
Serves: 6

RED BEANS AND PORK CHOPS

My grandmother grew up in New Orleans and she loved to cook red beans and rice. I'm talking about the red beans and rice that simmer all day long and at least to me as a young girl, seemed to be an awful lot of work. This dish is simple to prepare but carries many of the same flavors from my childhood. I love the addition of the pork chops. This is definitely the type of meal that will "stick to your ribs" and leave you full. Serve over rice with a side of corn bread.

Directions:

1. Add the oil in the inner pot, press the sauté button and adjust to brown mode. Season pork chops with celery salt and pepper and then brown on both sides in the inner pot. Remove and place onto a plate. Add the onions, garlic, pepper flakes, tomatoes, red beans, bay leaf, crab boil and sauté until the vegetables are soft and fragrant.

2. Provide a space on the center of the inner pot for the ham hock, level the surface with a wooden spoon and cover ingredients with the browned pork chops. Pour the stock in the pot and close the lid securely. Rotate the handle to lock the pressure cooker, position the steam

vent handle to sealing position and adjust to meat/stew mode.

3. Cook until the Instant Pot® switches to keep warm mode and release the pressure naturally until the floating valve drops down. Remove the ham hock and rinse with cool running water, close the lid and reset the pressure cooker to soup mode. Adjust cooking time to 10 minutes and cook it while preparing the ham hocks.
4. Remove the meat from the hocks and chop into small pieces. Return the shredded ham into the inner pot when the pressure cooker has switched to keep warm mode. Adjust seasoning according to preferred taste and let it stand in the pressure cooker before serving.
5. Portion the beans, shredded meat and pork chops into individual serving bowls and serve immediately.

Ingredients:

- 2 cups of canned red beans, drained
- 1 white onion, diced
- 1 tablespoon of oil
- 4 garlic cloves, minced
- 1 ½ cup of canned tomatoes with green chili peppers
- 1 bay leaf
- 1 teaspoon dry crab boil
- 1 teaspoon of celery salt
- ½ teaspoon of red pepper flakes, crushed
- 1 smoked pork knuckle (ham hock)
- ½ teaspoon of crushed peppercorns, to taste
- 4 1-inch thick pork chops, boneless

Preparation time: 15 minutes
Cooking time: 1 hour 30 minutes
Serves: 4

ROASTED PORK WITH FENNEL

Fennel has such a unique flavor that I really recommend you try this dish. The pork is seasoned to perfection, juicy and tender. The leftover stock makes the perfect gravy, just simmer until you've reached the consistency you prefer.

Directions:

1. Season pork with salt, pepper, garlic powder and onion powder and rub evenly on all areas. Add the oil in the inner pot, press the sauté button and adjust to brown mode. Add the pork to the inner pot and brown evenly on all sides. Remove pork from the pot and add the garlic, sauté until soft and fragrant.
2. Pour in white wine and stock and then stir the mixture while scraping the browned bits on the bottom of the inner pot. Bring to a boil and return the pork, close the lid securely and rotate the handle to lock the pressure cooker.
3. Reset the Instant Pot® and adjust to meat/stew mode and cook until it switches to keep warm mode. Release the pressure naturally until the floater valve drops down. Open the lid and stir in the onion slices and fennel, close the lid again but with steam vent in venting position. Set the cooking time to 10 minutes and cook until the vegetables are soft and cooked through.
4. Remove the vegetables and meat from the inner pot and cook the sauce further if you want a thicker sauce.
5. Portion the meat and vegetables into individual serving bowls, pour the sauce into each bowl and serve immediately.

Ingredients:

- 2 tablespoons of cooking oil
- 2 pounds of pork Boston butt, trimmed
- Salt and crushed peppercorns, to taste
- 1 teaspoon garlic powder
- 1 teaspoon onion powder
- ½ cup of white wine
- 1 cup of chicken stock
- 1 medium onion, halved and thinly sliced
- 1 pound of fennel bulbs, sliced

Preparation time: 20 minutes
Cooking time: 1 hour 20 minutes
Serves: 4

Beef

BBQ BEEF SHORT RIBS

The first time I had these short ribs I think I day dreamed about them for the next week. I'm pretty sure that anytime you combine honey, soy sauce and sugar some kind of magic happens. Don't waste another day before trying out this little bit of heaven!

Directions:

1. Combine together all sauce ingredients in a bowl and mix thoroughly until well incorporated. Season beef with salt and pepper and rub evenly on all areas.
2. Add the oil in the inner pot, press the sauté button and adjust to brown mode. Add the beef and brown evenly on all sides, turning occasionally for even searing. Pour in the sauce mixture and toss to coat the beef evenly with sauce. Close the lid, position steam vent handle to sealing position and reset the pressure cooker to meat/stew mode. Adjust to more/high heat and set the cooking time to 10 minutes. When the Instant Pot® switches to keep warm mode, reset to meat/stew mode and adjust to less/low heat. Set to 15 minutes cooking time and cook until the pressure cooker has switched to keep warm mode. Release the pressure naturally until the floater valve drops down. Let it stand in the pressure cooker to keep it warm before serving.
3. Open lid and remove the beef ribs from the inner pot. Transfer to a serving dish and serve immediately.

Ingredients:

- 1 rack of beef short rib (about 2 pounds), chopped into 1-rib portions
- 1 tablespoon of cooking oil
- Salt and pepper

For the Sauce

- 3 tablespoons of light soy sauce
- 3 tablespoons of raw cane sugar
- 2 tablespoons of honey
- 1 tablespoon of minced garlic
- 4 tablespoons of barbecue sauce
- 3 tablespoons of minced red onions
- 2 tablespoons of dark molasses
- 2 tablespoons of white vinegar
- 1 tablespoon of hot chili sauce

Preparation time: 10 minutes
Cooking time: 30 minutes
Serves: 4

BEEF BOURGUIGNON

Beef Bourguignon is a hearty, French stew that although difficult to spell, is surprisingly easy to create in your Instant Pot®. I love the flavor that the bacon brings to this dish. This meal is warm and comforting. It's traditionally served over mashed potatoes or egg noodles.

Directions:

1. Add the bacon into the inner pot, press the sauté button and adjust to brown mode. When the bacon has released some oil, add the onion and garlic and then sauté until soft. Add the meat and brown evenly on all sides while turning occasionally with a tong. Slowly add the flour while stirring regularly and cook until lightly browned. Pour in the wine and beef stock, add the seasoning ingredients and stir just to combine.
2. Close the lid securely, position stem vent handle to sealing position. Press the meat/stew button and set the cooking time to 20 minutes. Once your Instant Pot® switches to keep warm mode, let the pressure release naturally until the float valve drops down.
3. Open the lid and add the carrots and mushrooms. Close the lid, reset and cook for another 5 minutes. After the final cooking process, let it stand for 10 minutes before serving.
4. Open lid, transfer the beef bourguignon to a serving bowl and serve immediately.

Ingredients:

- 2 pounds of beef round steak, cut into 2-cm cubes
- Salt and ground pepper, to taste
- 1 cup of red wine
- ½ cup of beef stock
- 2 medium carrots, peeled and sliced into ½-inch rounds
- 4 slices of smoked bacon, diced
- 1 cup of fresh mushrooms, halved or quartered
- 2 tablespoons of sifted flour
- 1 large white onion, diced
- ½ teaspoon of dried basil leaves
- 1 teaspoon of minced garlic

Preparation time: 25 minutes
Cooking time: 35 minutes
Serves: 5 to 6

ONION-MUSHROOMS BEEF TIPS

Simple to prepare, but a very flavorful dish to eat. The beef cooks in a gravy sauce making it so tender and savory. On a weeknight, just toss together a quick salad, serve over egg noodles and you have an effortless meal.

Directions:

1. Add the oil in the inner pot, press the sauté button and adjust to brown mode. Season beef with salt and pepper and brown in oil, searing evenly on all sides in the inner pot. Stir in the onions and garlic and sauté for about 1 minute and then add the mushrooms, beef gravy and the stock.
2. Close the lid and reset the pressure cooker and press the meat/stew button. Position the steam vent to sealing position and set the cooking time to 20 minutes.
3. When the Instant Pot® switches to keep warm mode, let the pressure release naturally until the floater valve drops down. Open lid and adjust seasoning and consistency according to preference.
4. Transfer in a serving bowl or portion into individual serving bowls. Serve immediately.

Ingredients:

- 2 pounds of beef stew meat, cut into cubes
- Salt and ground pepper
- 2 tablespoons of cooking oil
- 2 cups of canned mushrooms, drained
- 2 cups of canned beef gravy
- 1 cup of sliced white onions
- 2 tablespoons garlic, minced
- ½ cup of brown beef stock

Preparation time: 10 minutes
Cooking time: 30 minutes
Serves: 8

BRAISED BEEF SHANKS

When I think of braised beef shanks I think of them being an option on the menu of a fancy restaurant. In reality, they are pretty easy to conquer right in your own home. The end result boasts a ton of flavor and makes for an impressive presentation.

Directions:

1. Season beef shanks with salt and pepper evenly on both sides. Tie each with twine to hold the meat together and retain its shape during the cooking process.
2. Add 1 tablespoon of oil to the inner pot, press the sauté button and sear half of the shanks evenly on both sides. Remove browned shanks and add the remaining oil. Put in the remaining beef shanks to the inner pot and brown evenly on both sides. Remove and transfer to a plate, set aside. Reserve 1 tablespoon of the cooking oil and drain the rest.
3. Add the onions, garlic, celery, carrots, thyme, 1 pinch of salt and the tomato paste in the inner pot and sauté until soft and fragrant. Pour in the stock and wine, and then cook until it reaches a boil while scraping the browned bits on the bottom of the inner pot. Return the beef shanks to the inner pot and add more stock if needed to cover the beef about halfway. Add the tomatoes and spread evenly over the beef.
4. Close the lid securely and rotate clockwise to close and lock the lid. Position the steam vent properly and press the meat/stew button. Cook for 30 minutes on high pressure.
5. When the Instant Pot® has completed the cooking process, let the pressure release naturally until the float valve drops down. Open the lid and skim the oil and bubbles off the top surface, transfer the beef to a serving platter and adjust sauce seasoning.

Ingredients:

- 2 tablespoon of cooking oil
- 6 pieces of 2-inch thick slices of beef shanks, excess fat trimmed
- 2 teaspoons of salt (for seasoning meat)
- 1 teaspoon of crushed black pepper (for seasoning meat)
- 1 medium onion, chopped
- 1 medium stalk of celery, chopped
- 1 large carrot, peeled and diced
- 3 garlic cloves, crushed
- 2 tablespoons of tomato paste
- 1 tablespoon of minced fresh thyme leaves
- ½ teaspoon of salt
- 1 to 2 cups of brown beef stock
- ½ cup of white wine
- 1 cup canned tomatoes, diced

For Serving

- ½ teaspoon of minced garlic
- ½ lemon, juiced and zested
- 1 cup loosely packed fresh parsley leaves, chopped

Preparation time: 10 minutes
Cooking time: 1 hour
Serves: 6

6. Pour the sauce over the braised meat.
7. Combine the ingredients used for serving and sprinkle it over the dish. Serve immediately.

POT ROAST

Pot roast can be a funny thing. I think people want to be nostalgic about it, but then they make it and it's a bit dry or the meat is tough, so it loses its appeal and therefore its' place at the dinner table. The key is learning how to correctly prepare a pot roast using this gem of a pressure cooker. It can work magic on most any meat, making it delicate and tender, worthy of the pot roasts we are longing for.

Directions:

1. Add the oil in the inner pot, press the sauté button and adjust to brown mode. Season beef with steak seasoning and rub evenly on all areas. Add the beef in the inner pot and brown on all sides, turning to brown the meat evenly. Remove the beef from the inner pot and set aside.
2. Add the onions and stock in the inner pot, place the steam rack inside the pot and place the beef on the basket. Close the lid securely and position steam vent to sealing position, reset to meat/stew mode and adjust to more/high mode.
3. When the Instant Pot® has completed the cooking process, let the pressure release naturally until the floater valve drops down. Open lid and remove the beef from the pot, transfer to a plate and cover with foil to keep it warm.
4. Add the flour-butter mixture into the pot with the cooking liquid and cook until thick while stirring constantly. When the flour mixture has dissolved completely, stir in the milk and season to taste with salt and pepper.
5. Place the pot roast on a serving platter, serve warm with gravy.

Ingredients:

- 3 pound beef chuck roast, cut into two portions
- 1 to 2 tablespoons of cooking oil
- 2 to 3 teaspoons of steak seasoning mix
- 2 cups of brown beef stock
- 1 tablespoon of dried onions
- 2 tablespoons of unsalted butter and 2 tablespoons of sifted flour mixture
- 4 tablespoon of milk, or as needed to adjust thickness

Preparation time: 10 minutes
Cooking time: 1 hour
Serves: 4

BEEF STROGANOFF

Beef stroganoff is a childhood favorite of mine. It brings back memories of doing homework in the kitchen while my mom prepared this dish on those cold Michigan nights. Luckily, with the Instant Pot®, I can deliver the same flavorful meal to my kids, but with little effort on my part. This leaves me more available to do fun things…like help with homework!

Directions:

1. Season the beef strips with salt and pepper and toss to evenly distribute the seasonings.
2. Add half of the oil into the inner pot and press the sauté button and adjust to brown mode. Add half of the meat into the inner pot and cook until browned evenly. Turn the meat with a tong occasionally while browning the meat. Remove from the inner pot, add the remaining oil and brown the remaining beef in the pot. Remove the meat and transfer to a plate.
3. Add the shallots in the pot and sauté until soft and tender. Stir in the mushrooms and cook until soft. Add the sherry, stock and tomato paste into the inner pot and stir to distribute the ingredients well. Return the meat into the pot, close the lid and rotate handle to lock the Instant Pot®. Position the steam vent to sealing position and reset the cooker by pressing the cancel button. Press the meat/stew button and adjust to more/high mode. Cook until the pressure cooker switches to keep warm mode.
4. Let the pressure release naturally until the float valve drops down. Let it stand for 10 minutes to finish the cooking process with low heat. Open the lid, stir in the sour cream and cook until warmed through.
5. Portion the cooked noodles into individual serving bowls, add the meat and vegetables on top and pour over the warm sauce. Sprinkle with paprika and serve immediately.

Ingredients:

- 1 ½ pounds of beef round steak, sliced into thin strips
- Salt and ground black pepper
- 3 tablespoons of cooking oil
- 2 tablespoons of minced shallot
- 1 cup of sliced mushrooms
- 4 tablespoons of dry sherry
- 2 cups beef stock
- 3 tablespoons of tomato paste
- ½ cup of sour cream, or as needed
- 1 pound of cooked egg noodles
- Sweet paprika, for serving

Preparation time: 10 minutes
Cooking time: 1 hour
Serves: 6 to 8

BEEF TENDERLOIN IN MUSHROOM SAUCE

Savory beef tenderloin is cooked with rustic mushrooms in a rich, creamy sauce. Adding the carrots and potatoes really makes this a one pot meal that is ready to eat whenever you are.

Directions:

1. Season the meat with salt and pepper and set aside.
2. Add the oil into the inner pot, press the sauté button and brown the meat in two batches. Transfer the browned meat to a dish or plate and set aside.
3. Add the onions, garlic, and carrots into the pot and pour in the red wine. Cook for 5 minutes while scraping the browned bits on the bottom of the inner pot. Return the browned meat and the remaining ingredients and briefly stir to combine. Season to taste with salt and pepper and then close the lid securely.
4. Rotate the lid handle clockwise to fully close and lock the lid. Position the steam release handle properly and press the meat/stew button, cook on high and set the time to 15 minutes.
5. When the Instant Pot® has completed the cooking process, let the steam release naturally until the float valve drops down. Let it stand for 10 minutes, or keep it warm in the pressure cooker for hours before serving. Adjust seasoning and cook further to thicken the sauce if desired.
6. Portion the beef and vegetables into individual serving bowls, pour in the sauce and serve warm.

Ingredients:

- 2 pounds of beef tenderloin, cut into cubes
- Salt and ground black pepper
- 2 tablespoons of cooking oil
- 1 cup of diced red onions
- 1 cup of diced carrots
- 1 teaspoon of minced garlic
- 1 cup cream of mushroom soup
- 1 cup of quartered or sliced shiitake mushrooms
- 1 cup of diced potatoes
- ½ cup of red wine
- 2 cups of brown beef stock
- 2 tablespoons of Worcestershire sauce

Preparation time: 10 minutes
Cooking time: 40 minutes
Serves: 8

TEX MEX BRISKET

This versatile dish has many uses. Serve just as it is, stick it between a bun, or serve on top of a salad. Anyway you go about it this brisket makes families happy.

Directions:

1. Combine together all marinade ingredients in a bowl and mix until the ingredients are well incorporated. Add the beef and rub evenly on all areas. Cover bowl and chill for at least 12 hours to allow the flavors to penetrate into the meat.
2. Add the oil into the inner pot, press the sauté button and brown the meat evenly on all sides. Lift the meat partially, add the tomatoes with its juice and spread evenly on the bottom of the inner pot. Position the meat on top of the tomatoes and close the lid.
3. Rotate the handle clockwise to close and lock the lid. Position the steam vent properly and press the meat/stew button, cook on medium for 45 to 60 minutes.
4. When your Instant Pot® has completed the cooking process, let the pressure release naturally until the float valve drops down. Remove the lid and turn to coat the other side with sauce. Close the lid and let it stand for 10 minutes.
5. Remove the meat and transfer on a cutting board, let it cool and slice the meat across the grain. Transfer to a serving dish, pour the sauce over the meat and serve.

Ingredients:

- 2 pounds of trimmed beef brisket
- 2 tablespoons of cooking oil
- 1 ½ cup of canned tomatoes, chopped
- 1 medium white onion, halved and thinly sliced

For the marinade

- 1 teaspoon of onion powder
- 1 teaspoon of garlic powder
- 1 jalapeno pepper, sliced
- 1 tablespoon of sugar
- 1 tablespoons of Worcestershire sauce
- 2 to 3 teaspoons of chili powder
- 2 tablespoons of lemon juice
- 1 teaspoon of ground cumin
- 1 teaspoon of salt
- ½ teaspoon of ground black pepper

Preparation time: 10 minutes, (12 hour marinade)
Cooking time: 1 hour, 20 minutes
Serves: 8

BEEF IN MOCHA SAUCE

This meat offers a surprising combination of flavors that are sure to wow your taste buds. Even if you want to eat the meat straight out of the pot, don't skip out on making the delectable sauce to pour on top of the meat. I promise, it's worth it!

Directions:

1. Combine all mocha rub ingredients in a bowl and mix until well combined. Divide the rub mixture and reserve half for the sauce. Add the beef into the bowl and toss to evenly coat with the rub mixture. Set aside.
2. Place all ingredients for the sauce (including reserved rub mixture) in a blender or food processor and pulse until a smooth consistency is achieved. Transfer to a bowl, set aside.
3. Add the oil to the inner pot, press the sauté button and add half of the beef. Brown the meat evenly on all sides. Remove from the inner pot and brown the remaining beef. Return the first batch of browned beef into the inner pot and pour in the sauce mixture.
4. Close the lid securely and rotate the handle clockwise to close and lock the lid. Position the steam vent properly to sealing position and press the meat/stew button. Cook with high pressure and set cooking time to 20 minutes.
5. When your Instant Pot® has completed the cooking process, let the pressure release naturally until the floater valve drops down. Let it stand for 10 minutes before opening the lid to continue the cooking process with low heat.
6. Open the lid and remove the meat from the inner pot. Place it in a large bowl and shred with two fork. Heat the sauce to thicken until the desired consistency is achieved. Pour in the sauce and toss to coat the shredded meat.
7. Transfer to a serving platter and serve warm.

Ingredients:

- 2 pounds lean beef meat, cut into cubes
- 2 tablespoons of cooking oil

For the Sauce

- 2 cups of brown beef stock
- 1 medium onion, diced
- 4 pieces of chopped, dried figs (soaked for 2 hours in the beef stock)
- 2 tablespoons of balsamic vinegar
- Salt and pepper, to taste

For the Mocha dry rub

- 1 ½ to 2 tablespoons of ground coffee
- 2 tablespoons of paprika
- 2 to 3 teaspoon of coarsely ground black pepper
- 2 teaspoons of cocoa powder
- 1 teaspoon of crushed red pepper flakes
- 1 teaspoon of chili powder
- 1 teaspoon of powdered ginger
- 1 teaspoon of table salt

Preparation time: 15 minutes
Cooking time: 45 minutes
Serves: 4

MEXICAN BEEF RECIPE

This is a kid pleasing dish that has a delicious, rich sauce for the meat. After you brown the beef, you pretty much just have to get the rest of the ingredients into the Instant Pot® and stand back and wait. Very simple, with delectable results.

Directions:

1. Combine together chili powder, salt and black pepper in a large bowl and add the beef. Toss to coat the meat and set aside.
2. Add the clarified butter or oil to the inner pot, press sauté and lightly brown the meat. Remove from the inner pot and transfer to a plate. Add the onions and garlic, sauté for 3 minutes until soft and fragrant and add the tomato paste. Stir in the fish sauce, tomato salsa and return the beef in the inner pot. Briefly stir to combine and close the lid.
3. Rotate the handle clockwise to lock the lid and position the steam vent properly to sealing position. Press the meat/stew button and set the cooking time to 30 minutes.
4. When your Instant Pot® has completed the cooking time, use the natural release method until the float valve drops down. Let it stand for 10 minutes before opening the lid to further cook the meat with low heat.
5. Open the lid and transfer the meat with the cooking sauce to a serving platter. Serve with minced cilantro on top.

Ingredients:

- 2 pounds lean beef meat or beef brisket, cut into 2-inch cubes
- 1 tablespoon of crushed red pepper flakes or chili powder
- 1 teaspoon of salt and ½ teaspoon ground black pepper
- 1 tablespoon clarified butter or cooking oil
- 1 red onion, halved and julienned
- 2 to 3 teaspoons of tomato paste
- 2 tablespoons of minced garlic
- ½ cup tomato salsa
- 1 cup of brown beef stock
- 1 teaspoon fish sauce
- 1 cup loosely packed fresh cilantro leaves, minced

Preparation time: 10 minutes
Cooking time: 1 hour
Serves: 8

BEEF SHORT RIBS WITH MASHED VEGETABLES

This is comfort food to me. A light, brothy sauce poured over meat that is so tender that it barely hangs on the bone served next to a perfectly seasoned pile of fluffy mashed potatoes and carrots. I really just want to put on my favorite comfy pants and curl up on the couch with this dish.

Directions:

1. Combine together the flour, salt and pepper in a large bowl until well combined and add the ribs. Coat the ribs evenly on all sides with the flour mixture. Set aside.
2. Add the oil to the inner pot, press the sauté button and brown the ribs in separate batches. Transfer the ribs to a plate and set aside. Add the garlic, onions, and thyme in the inner pot and sauté until soft and fragrant. Pour in the wine and stock, bring to a boil and stir while scraping the browned bits on the bottom of the pan.
3. Return the ribs to the inner pot and arrange them in a way that all are evenly covered with the cooking liquid. Add the potatoes and carrots in the steamer basket and place it over the beef in the inner pot. Close the lid securely and rotate the handle clockwise to lock the lid. Position the steam vent properly to sealing position, press the meat/stew button and set the cooking time to 45 minutes.
4. When the Instant Pot® has completed the cooking time, use the natural release method until the float valve drops down. Let it stand for 10 minutes to further cook the ribs with low heat.
5. Open the lid and remove the steam tray with vegetables and transfer into a bowl. Mash the potatoes and carrots and melt in the butter. Season with salt and pepper and mix until well combined.
6. Transfer the ribs to a serving platter, drizzle with cooking sauce and serve with mashed vegetables.

Preparation time: 30 minutes
Cooking time: 1 hour, 15 minutes
Serves: 6

Ingredients:

- 2 tablespoons butter, for the mashed vegetables
- 1 tablespoon of cooking oil
- 3 tablespoon of sifted flour
- 3 pounds of beef short ribs or about 6 ribs
- 1 teaspoon salt and 1 teaspoon ground pepper, to taste
- 1 medium white onion, minced
- 1 teaspoon minced garlic
- 1 sprig fresh thyme leaves, chopped
- ½ cup of red wine
- ½ brown beef stock
- 2 medium potatoes, diced
- 2 large carrots, diced

Beef Short Ribs With Mashed Vegetables

MONGOLIAN BEEF

The flavor of this dish is ah-mazing! Like the type of amazing that if there are even any leftovers you will want to wake up in the middle of the night and eat them before anyone else in your family has the chance. Ok, I don't really do this, but you should really try this dish soon! I like to serve the beef over rice with a side of stir fry veggies.

Directions:

1. Place the meat in a large bowl and season with salt, pepper, onion powder and garlic powder.
2. Add the oil to the inner pot, press the sauté button and brown the meat in 2 batches. Transfer the meat to a plate and set aside. Add the garlic and ginger in the inner pot and sauté until lightly browned and fragrant. Stir in the sugar, soy sauce and beef stock and return the beef into the inner pot.
3. Close the lid securely and rotate the handle to lock the lid. Position the steam vent properly to sealing position, press the meat/stew button and set the cooking time to 15 minutes.
4. When your Instant Pot® has completed the cooking time, use natural release method until the float valve drops down. Let it stand for 10 minutes to further cook the meat with low heat.
5. Stir the cornstarch-water mixture and pour it in the inner pot. Press sauté and cook until the sauce is thick and heated through. Press the cancel button to stop the cooking process.
6. Transfer to a serving bowl and serve with sliced green onions on top.

Ingredients:

- 2 pounds of skirt or flank steak, sliced into thin strips
- Salt and ground black pepper
- ½ teaspoon garlic powder
- ½ teaspoon onion powder
- 1 tablespoon of cooking oil
- 1 teaspoon of minced garlic
- ½ cup of tamari soy or light soy sauce
- 1/2 of cup of beef stock
- ½ cup of packed raw cane sugar
- 1-inch piece of fresh ginger root, minced
- 2 tablespoons cornstarch and 3 tablespoons water, thickener
- 3 stems of green onions, sliced

Preparation time: 10 minutes
Cooking time: 45 minutes
Serves: 8

CHILI BEEF BURRITOS

My family loves to eat tacos. Hard shells, soft shells, or taco salad. It doesn't matter how it is served to them, if it is topped with some delicious meat and a generous sprinkling of cheese, they will eat it. There is still a bit of a debate on whether sour cream is a welcome addition to a taco or not, but I digress. Prepare this chili beef burritos recipe for your family tonight and soon they will be singing their taco praises to you.

Directions:

1. Add the oil into the inner cooking pot of the pressure cooker, and then swirl to coat the sides of the pot. Add one tortilla at a time and lightly brown on both sides. Transfer on a plate set aside.
2. Add the beef, half of the enchilada sauce, chili sauce, beef bouillon and the stock in the inner pot and stir to combine.
3. Close the lid securely and rotate the handle to lock the lid. Position the steam vent properly to sealing position, press the meat/stew button and set the cooking time to 30 minutes. When your Instant Pot® has completed the cooking time, use natural release method until the float valve drops down. Let it stand for 10 minutes to further cook with low heat.
4. Open the lid, add the remaining enchilada sauce and cook until heated through. Remove the meat and transfer to a bowl. Remove the sauce and transfer to a separate bowl.
5. Add about ½ cup of beef to each tortilla, spoon over with the sauce and top with shredded cheese and the optional toppings. Fold in both sides of tortillas and roll it upwards to secure the stuffing. Repeat the procedure with the remaining ingredients.
6. Slice each burrito into two portions or serve whole.

Ingredients:

- 2 pounds of beef round steak, cut into cubes or thinly sliced across the grain
- 1 teaspoon cooking oil
- 1 ½ cups of enchilada sauce, divided
- 2 tablespoons of chili sauce
- 1 beef bouillon cube
- 1 cup brown beef stock
- 8 to 10 flour tortillas
- 2 cups of shredded Cheddar cheese
- Diced tomatoes (optional)
- Shredded lettuce (optional)
- Avocado slices (optional)

Preparation time: 10 minutes
Cooking time: 45 minutes
Serves: 6 to 8

Poultry

CHICKEN CACCIATORE

The word "cacciatore" means hunter in Italian and this dish is essentially prepared hunter style with plenty of garlic, mushrooms, onions, peppers. This meal is rustic like a chicken stew only it is served with large pieces of chicken mixed with vegetables in a tomato inspired sauce.

Directions:

1. Combine together the flour, salt, black pepper and smoked paprika in a bowl and add the chicken. Toss to coat the chicken evenly with flour mixture.
2. Add 1 tablespoon of oil in the inner pot, press the sauté button and brown the chicken in two batches. Remove from the inner pot and transfer to a plate.
3. Add the remaining oil in the inner pot and sauté the onion, garlic, green pepper and tomatoes for 4 minutes. Add the tomato paste, chicken stock and return the chicken.
4. Close the lid securely and rotate the handle to lock the lid. Position the steam vent properly to sealing position, press the chicken button and set the cooking time to 10 minutes.
5. When the Instant Pot® has completed the cooking time, release the pressure using the natural release method until the float valve drops down. Open the lid and stir in the mushrooms and hot chili sauce to taste, cook until it returns to a boil.
6. Remove the chicken with slotted spoon and place into a serving bowl. Pour in the sauce and serve immediately.

Ingredients:

- 3 tablespoons of sifted flour
- 1 teaspoon of salt
- 1 teaspoon of smoked paprika
- ½ teaspoon of black pepper
- 3 to 4 pounds of whole chicken, cut into 8 or 12 portions
- 2 tablespoons of cooking oil
- 1 large green sweet pepper, sliced into strips
- 1 white onion, diced
- 2 cloves of garlic, minced
- 1 cup canned tomatoes, diced
- 1 cup chicken stock
- ½ cup tomato paste
- 1 cup of quartered mushrooms
- Hot chili sauce, to taste

Preparation time: 10 minutes
Cooking time: 35 minutes
Serves: 6

TURKEY WITH ORANGE-WHISKEY SAUCE

Now you can serve turkey on any ordinary day and make it memorable by smothering it in a delectable orange-whiskey sauce. Suddenly, the day is anything but ordinary. I love that the ingredient list is straightforward and probably things you already have on hand.

Directions:

1. Season the turkey with salt and pepper and rub evenly on all sides.
2. Add 2 tablespoons of clarified butter and press the sauté button. Once the clarified butter is hot, brown the turkey skin-side down and turn to brown the other side. Remove from the inner pot and transfer to a plate.
3. Melt 2 tablespoons of unsalted butter and stir in whiskey, stock, orange juice, orange zest and cayenne pepper in the inner pot and bring it to a boil. Return the turkey to the inner pot and baste with sauce.
4. Close the lid securely and rotate the handle to lock the lid. Position the steam vent properly to sealing position, press the poultry button and set the cooking time to 20 minutes.
5. When the Instant Pot® has completed the cooking process, use the natural release method to release the pressure until the floater valve drops down. Open the lid and remove the turkey and transfer it to a plate. Let it stand for 10 minutes before slicing.
6. If the sauce is not yet thick, cook further until the desired consistency is achieved. Pour the sauce over the sliced turkey and serve immediately.

Ingredients:

- 2 tablespoons of clarified butter
- 1 turkey breast with skin, brined
- Salt and ground black pepper
- 1 cup of chicken stock
- 2 tablespoons of unsalted butter
- 3 tablespoons honey
- ¼ cup of whiskey
- 1 tablespoon grated orange rind
- 2 tablespoons orange juice
- 1 teaspoon of cayenne pepper

Preparation time: 10 minutes
Cooking time: 1 hour 15 minutes
Serves: 4

TURKEY BREAST IN ORANGE-CRANBERRY SAUCE

In my kitchen, turkey and cranberry go together like peas and carrots, peanut butter and jelly or Mario and Luigi. You just can't have one without the other. The orange is a welcome addition to the cranberry, giving it a slight citrus flavor. I love that the sauce is light and fruity. It's a nice change from the usual turkey gravies that are thick and heavy.

Directions:

1. Combine together the orange juice, cranberry jelly and onion soup mix in the inner pot and season to taste with salt and pepper. Add the turkey breast skin-side down and close the lid securely.
2. Rotate the handle clockwise to lock the lid and position the steam vent properly to sealing position. Press the poultry button and set the cooking time to 25 minutes.
3. When your Instant Pot® has completed the cooking process, let the pressure release naturally until the float valve drops down. Let it stand for 10 minutes to further cook with low heat. Open the lid, remove the turkey and transfer to a plate. Slice or carve the breast according to preferred thickness and set aside.
4. If the sauce is not yet thick, cook further until the desired consistency is achieved and transfer to a bowl.
5. Serve the carved turkey warm with the sauce in a separate bowl.

Ingredients:

- 3 to 4 pounds of turkey breast
- Salt and black pepper, to taste
- 2 ½ to 3 cups fresh orange juice
- 1 cup of cranberry jelly
- 1 package or homemade onion soup mix

Preparation time: 10 minutes
Cooking time: 45 minutes
Serves: 8

SEASONED WHOLE CHICKEN

When I first started cooking I would see recipes for whole chickens and I would immediately get intimidated and keep looking. After gathering my courage and trying my first whole chicken I realized that they are not only extremely tasty, they are quite simple to prepare, too. If this is your first attempt at cooking the whole chicken, I recommend you give this recipe a try. It's very beginner friendly and full of flavor.

Directions:

1. Combine together the salt, black pepper, smoked paprika and dried thyme in a bowl and rub it evenly on all sides of the chicken.
2. Add the oil in the inner pot, press the sauté button and brown the chicken evenly on all sides. Pour in the stock, lemon juice and add in the garlic.
3. Close the lid securely and rotate the handle to lock the lid. Position the steam vent properly to the sealing position, press the poultry button and set the cooking time to 25 minutes.
4. When your Instant Pot® has completed the cooking process, release the pressure using the natural release method until the float valve drops down. Let it stand to further cook with low heat and open the lid. Remove chicken from the inner pot and transfer to a serving platter.
5. Carve into portions or serve whole.

Ingredients:

- 1 whole chicken or about 3 to 4 pounds
- 1 tablespoon of cooking oil
- 1 teaspoon of smoked paprika
- 1 ½ cups of chicken stock
- 1 teaspoon of dried thyme leaves
- ½ teaspoon of table salt
- ½ teaspoon of crushed black pepper
- 1 lemon, juiced
- 4 garlic cloves, crushed and peeled

Preparation time: **10** minutes
Cooking time: **35** minutes
Serves: **10**

CHICKEN THIGHS

Chicken thighs are so yummy and easy peasy prepared this way. The sauce is light and doesn't get super thick like gravy so I love to pair it with small red potatoes that have been either boiled or roasted.

Directions:

1. Season the chicken with salt and pepper and rub evenly on all sides.
2. Add the oil in the inner pot, press the sauté button and brown the chicken evenly on both sides. Remove from the inner pot and transfer to a plate.
3. Add the onions and garlic into the inner pot and sauté until soft and fragrant. Add the mushrooms, chicken stock and wine. Return the chicken into the inner pot and close the lid securely.
4. Rotate the handle to lock the lid and position the steam release properly to sealing position. Press the poultry button and set the cooking time to 10 minutes.
5. When the Instant Pot® has completed the cooking process, release the pressure using the natural release method until the float valve drops down. Open the lid and transfer the chicken to a plate. Stir the flour and water mixture and pour it into the inner pot. Cook for about 5 minutes or until the sauce has thickened, season to taste and transfer to a bowl.
6. Serve the chicken with the sauce in a separate bowl or pour on top. Serve over small potatoes or egg noodles.

Ingredients:

- 4 pieces of chicken thighs, deboned
- Salt and ground black pepper, to taste
- 1/2 cup of diced white onions
- 1 teaspoon of minced garlic
- 1 tablespoon of cooking oil
- ½ cup of halved mushrooms
- 1/4 cup of white wine
- 1 cup of chicken stock
- 2 tablespoons of cornstarch and 3 tablespoon water (to thicken sauce)

Preparation time: 10 minutes
Cooking time: 20 minutes
Serves: 4

THAI CHICKEN THIGHS

Two confessions. The first is that when I was just getting comfortable in the kitchen I would see a Thai recipe and think, "No way, I'm sure that's way too hard and has too many exotic ingredients." I wouldn't even consider preparing it. And after I finally felt like maybe it was something I could attempt, I looked at the ingredient list and thought, "Peanut butter and lime juice? Soy sauce and cilantro? How can anything tasty come out of this weird pairing of ingredients?" I was wrong on both accounts. This recipe is very simple. If you can add a few ingredients to your Instant Pot® then you can make these Thai chicken thighs. And just so you know. All those crazy ingredients? Pure magic when mixed together. I hope you enjoy!

Directions:

1. Season the chicken with salt and black pepper and rub evenly on all sides.
2. Add the oil to the inner pot, press the sauté button and brown the chicken in separate batches. Return the browned chicken to the inner pot and add in the stock,, soy sauce, peanut butter, lime juice, crushed red pepper, cilantro and powdered ginger. Briefly stir to combine and close the lid securely.
3. Rotate the handle to lock the lid and position the steam handle properly to sealing position. Press the poultry button and set the cooking time to 10 minutes.
4. When the Instant Pot® has completed the cooking process, release the pressure naturally until the float valve drops down. Open the lid and remove the chicken, transfer to a bowl and set aside.
5. Stir the corn starch-water mixture and add it into the inner pot with cooking liquid. Cook for about 5 minutes and bring to a boil, or until the sauce has thickened while stirring regularly. Return the chicken and coat with sauce.
6. Transfer to a bowl and serve warm with chopped peanuts and onions on top.

Ingredients:

- 1 tablespoon of cooking oil
- Salt and black pepper, to taste
- 2 pounds of chicken thighs, deboned and skin removed
- 1 cup of chicken stock
- 3 tablespoons of peanut butter
- 3 tablespoons of light soy sauce
- 2 teaspoons of dried cilantro leaves
- juice of 1 lime
- ½ teaspoon of crushed red pepper flakes
- 1 teaspoon of ginger powder
- 1 tablespoon of corn starch and 2 tablespoons water mixed, thickener
- 3 tablespoons of chopped dry-roasted peanuts
- 2 stems of chopped green onions, for serving

Preparation time: 10 minutes
Cooking time: 25 minutes
Serves: 4 to 6

GREEN CHILE WITH CHICKEN

I know that the ingredient list is long on this one. But authentic, crazy good Mexican food doesn't come together without a few of these ingredients. If you don't mind a little choppin' and preparin' you will have yourself one delicious meal when you are through. Invite some friends over for dinner or eat it all yourself. I won't tell.

Directions:

1. Add the oil into the inner pot, press the sauté button and add the onions and garlic. Sauté until soft and add the chicken, the peppers, cumin seeds, tomatillos, jalapeno, salt and the stock.
2. Close the lid securely and rotate the handle to lock the lid. Position the steam handle properly to sealing position, press the poultry button and set the cooking time to 15 minutes.
3. When your Instant Pot® has completed the cooking process, let the pressure release naturally until the float valve drops down. Open the lid, remove the chicken with a thong and transfer to a plate. Remove the bones and skin of the chicken and discard.
4. Add the cilantro and fish sauce into the inner pot and transfer the mixture into a food processor. Pulse the mixture until smooth, transfer to a bowl or serving platter and add the shredded chicken.
5. Serve warm with chopped cilantro on top with tortillas and lime wedges on the sides.

Ingredients:

- 2 pounds of chicken drumsticks
- 1 teaspoon of oil
- 2 tomatillos, husk removed and quartered
- 2 Poblano peppers, seeded and diced
- ¼ cup chopped sweet red peppers
- 2 jalapeños, chopped
- 1 large yellow onion, diced
- 4 garlic cloves, crushed and peeled
- 2 teaspoons of toasted cumin seeds (can substitute 1-2 teaspoons cumin powder)
- ½ cup chicken stock
- ¼ teaspoon of salt, to taste
- ½ cup of chopped fresh cilantro leaves
- 2 teaspoons of fish sauce
- 4 to 6 corn tortillas, for serving
- 1 lime, sliced into wedges, for serving

Preparation time: 10 minutes
Cooking time: 25 minutes
Serves: 4

CHICKEN AND CHICKPEA MASALA

Do you know what I love about the Instant Pot® pressure cooker? I can make a meal in under an hour that tastes like I've been simmering it on the stove all day. It must work really hard to develop so much flavor in such a short amount of time. This dish offers intense flavors that are both decadent and comforting all at once. I know the spice list is long, but I'll almost guarantee you have many of them in your cabinet already.

Directions:

1. Add the ghee into the inner cooking pot of the pressure cooker and press the sauté button. When the ghee is hot, sauté the garlic, onions and ginger for 5 minutes, or until lightly brown and aromatic. Stir in the pepper, cayenne/chili powder, cumin, smoked paprika, turmeric and coriander and cook for 1 minute. Add the tomatoes and spinach and cook for about 3 minutes or until the spinach is wilted.
2. Add in the chicken, half of the chopped cilantro and pour in the stock. Season to taste with salt and pepper and then close and lock the lid securely. Position the steam release handle to sealing position and pressure cook on high for 20 minutes.
3. When the Instant Pot® has completed the cooking cycle, quick release the pressure until the float valve drops down. Open the lid and stir in the cream, chickpeas and lemon juice into the inner cooking pot and cook until it returns to a simmer while stirring regularly.
4. Transfer to a serving bowl, top with the remaining chopped cilantro and then serve immediately.

Ingredients:

- 2 tablespoons of ghee/clarified butter
- 1 red onion, coarsely chopped
- 2 teaspoon of minced garlic
- 1-inch piece of fresh ginger root, minced or grated
- ½ tablespoon of cumin powder
- ½ tablespoon of smoked paprika
- ½ tablespoon of coriander powder
- ½ tablespoon of turmeric powder
- ½ teaspoon of chili powder or cayenne pepper, as needed to taste
- ½ teaspoon of crushed black pepper
- 2 cups of canned tomatoes
- 2 cups of packed fresh spinach leaves, trimmed and chopped
- 3 to 4 tablespoons of fresh lemon juice
- ½ cup loosely packed fresh cilantro leaves, chopped
- 1 ½ pounds chicken drumsticks
- 1 ½ pounds of chicken thighs
- 1 cup of chicken stock
- 2 cups of canned garbanzo/chickpeas, drained
- ½ cup of heavy cream (or coconut milk)
- Table salt, to taste

Preparation time: 10 minutes Cooking time: 30 minutes Serves: 4

HAWAIIAN BBQ CHICKEN

It doesn't get much simpler than this meal for a busy night. You can use fresh or canned pineapple, and any type of boneless chicken. I like to use a mixture of chicken thighs and chicken tenders.

Directions:

1. Combine together the BBQ sauce, coconut milk, and chili flakes. Add the chicken and toss to evenly coat with the sauce mixture. Set aside.
2. In the inner pot of your Instant Pot®, place the pineapples and spread evenly on the bottom. Place the chicken pieces over the pineapples and pour over the remaining sauce on top.
3. Close the lid completely and position steam release handle to sealing position.
4. Press the manual button and set the pressure cooking time to 10 minutes.
5. When the pressure cooking cycle is completed, slide the steam release handle to venting position to fully release the pressure. Open the lid when the float valve has dropped down. Remove the chicken with a pair of tongs and cook the sauce further in sauté mode until it has thickened.
6. Return the chicken and gently toss to evenly coat with the sauce mixture.
7. Transfer to serving bowl or platter and serve immediately with lime wedges.

Ingredients:

- 3 pounds of boneless chicken in small strips
- salt and pepper, to taste
- 1 teaspoon of chili flakes or powder
- 1 cup of sweet honey BBQ sauce
- 2 cups of pineapple chunks
- 1 cup low fat canned coconut milk or cream
- 2 limes, sliced into wedges for serving

Preparation time: 10 minutes
Cooking time: 10 minutes
Serves: 6-8

CHICKEN A LA KING

This dish is not only tasty (which is, of course, the most important part) but it makes an appealing presentation because of all of the colorful vegetables. The sauce is rich and creamy. I like to serve it over egg noodles, but know many people who enjoy it over biscuits.

Directions:

1. Combine all ingredients except for the pea and pimientos in the inner pot and stir to combine. Close the lid securely and rotate the handle to lock the lid. Position the steam handle properly to sealing position, press the poultry button and set the cooking time to 15 minutes.
2. When the Instant Pot® has completed the cooking process, let the pressure release naturally until the float valve drops down. Open the lid, remove the chicken and transfer to a plate. Cut into bite size pieces and set aside.
3. Add the peas and pimientos to the inner pot with the cooking sauce and cook until the sauce has thickened while stirring regularly. Return the chicken to the inner pot and cook until heated through.
4. Portion into individual serving bowls and serve warm.

Ingredients:

- 2 tablespoons of clarified butter
- 4 pieces chicken breasts, deboned and skin removed
- 1 medium green bell pepper, diced
- 1 medium white onion, diced
- 2 medium stalks of celery, diced
- ½ cup of button mushrooms, quartered
- 1 cup of canned mushroom soup
- 1 teaspoon of crushed dried tarragon
- Salt and ground black pepper, to taste
- 1 cup of white wine
- 2 cup of chicken stock
- 1 cup of water
- 1 cup of canned peas, for serving
- 2 tablespoons of canned/jarred pimientos, minced, for serving

Preparation time: 10 minutes
Cooking time: 30 minutes
Serves: 4

CHICKEN WITH SHERRY, MUSTARD & OLIVES

Did you see olives and immediately want to pass on preparing this dish? Or perhaps you love olives and were excited to see them make an appearance? Either way, don't miss out on this dish! If you aren't an olive fan, the chicken and sauce alone are delightful. Or you could make a substitution for the olives such as tiny button mushrooms or extra herbs like thyme or basil. If you love olives, they will shine here adding so much zip and tang to the sauce that you will not be disappointed.

Directions:

1. Add the oil to the inner pot, press the sauté button and brown the chicken in separate batches. Return all the chicken in the inner pot, add the onions, mustard, sherry wine, stock and wine vinegar in the inner pot and stir to combine.
2. Close the lid securely and rotate the handle to lock the lid. Position the steam vent properly to sealing position, press the poultry button and set the cooking time to 15 minutes.
3. When the pressure cooker has completed the cooking process, let the pressure release naturally until the float valve drops down.
4. Open the lid, stir in the olives and parsley and cook until heated through.
5. Transfer into a serving bowl and serve immediately.

Ingredients:

- 2 tablespoons of cooking oil
- 4 chicken breasts
- 4 red onions, quartered
- 1 tablespoon of Dijon mustard
- ½ cup of sherry wine
- 1 cup of chicken stock
- 2 teaspoons of red wine vinegar
- ½ cup of stuffed green olives
- ½ cup loosely packed fresh parsley leaves, chopped
- Salt and black pepper, to taste

Preparation time: 10 minutes
Cooking time: 25 minutes
Serves: 4

TURKEY WITH GRAVY

Turkey is an excellent source of lean protein. And who doesn't love a turkey sandwich made with real turkey, not processed lunchmeat? Use this easy recipe to prepare a scrumptious turkey dinner and then use the leftovers for sandwiches the next day.

Directions:

1. Season turkey with salt and pepper and rub evenly on all sides. Add the clarified butter in the inner pot, press the sauté button and brown the breast evenly on both sides. Remove from the inner pot and set aside.
2. Add the onions, garlic, carrots, sage and celery and sauté until soft and fragrant and pour in the stock and white wine. Cook for about 5 minutes until it has reduced slightly and return the turkey to the inner pot skin-side up.
3. Close the lid securely and rotate the handle clockwise to lock the lid. Position the steam handle properly to sealing position, press the poultry button and set the cooking time to 30 minutes.
4. When the Instant Pot® has completed the cooking process, let the pressure release naturally until the float valve drops down. Open the lid, remove the turkey and transfer to a plate wrapped in foil. After 10 minutes, slice the breast into ½ inch-thick pieces and set aside.
5. Transfer the cooking liquid into a food processor and pulse until smooth. Return to the inner pot and add the cornstarch. Cook until the sauce has thickened while stirring regularly and season to taste with salt and pepper. Switch off the Instant Pot® and transfer the gravy to a bowl.
6. Serve the turkey breast warm with gravy in a serving bowl.

Ingredients:

- 1 turkey breast
- Salt and black pepper, to taste
- 2 tablespoons of clarified butter
- 1 cup of diced white onions
- 1 cup of diced carrots
- ½ cup of chopped celery
- 2 garlic cloves, crushed and peeled
- 1 tablespoon chopped sage leaves
- 3 tablespoons of white wine
- 1 ½ cups of chicken stock
- 1 bay leaf
- 1 tablespoon cornstarch

Preparation time: 15 minutes
Cooking time: 1 hour
Serves: 6

CHICKEN WITH CHORIZO AND CHICKPEAS IN TOMATO SAUCE

At least for my family, adding sausage to a recipe instantly elevates it to a higher level of yumminess. This recipe is no exception. Combine that fact with a sauce consisting of roasted tomatoes and crunchy chickpeas and this dish is a clear winner. And its kid friendly, too!

Directions:

1. Add the oil in the inner pot, press the sauté button and add the chorizo and cook until lightly browned. Stir in the onions, sauté until soft and add in the chickpeas, tomatoes, smoke paprika, chicken, wine vinegar and the stock. Season to taste with salt and pepper and close the lid securely.
2. Rotate the handle clockwise to lock the lid and position the steam handle properly to the sealing position. Press the poultry button and set the cooking time to 15 minutes.
3. When your Instant Pot® has completed the cooking process, let the pressure release naturally until the float valve drops down. Let it stand for 10 minutes to further cook the chicken with low heat.
4. Open the lid, stir in the parsley and adjust the seasoning if needed.
5. Transfer to a serving bowl and serve immediately.

Ingredients:

- 2 tablespoons of cooking oil
- 4 links of Spanish smoked chorizo, casings removed and chopped
- 1 white onion, sliced into strips
- 2 teaspoons of smoked paprika
- 1 cup of canned chickpeas, drained
- 2 cups of canned roasted tomatoes
- 3 to 4 pounds whole chicken, cut into 8 portions (or substitute 5-6 boneless, skinless chicken breasts and thighs)
- 2 cups of chicken stock
- Salt and crushed black pepper, to taste
- 1 tablespoon of red wine vinegar
- Fresh parsley, chopped for serving

Preparation time: 10 minutes
Cooking time: 30 minutes
Serves: 6

CHICKEN THIGHS WITH ARTICHOKES

This recipe features beautiful colors and flavors, plus it's packed with veggies. My kids will even eat this one! Experiment with your favorite seasoning to make it your own. I like to serve with long grain and wild rice.

Directions:

1. Add the oil to the inner pot and press the sauté button. Sprinkle salt, pepper and garlic powder all over both sides of the chicken thighs. Add the chicken to the pot and brown, in batches if necessary. When all are browned remove and place on a plate.
2. Use 1 tbsp. of chicken broth to deglaze the pot, scraping at all the browned bits. Add 1 tsp olive oil to the pot and pour in the onions and the carrots. Sauté until the onions just begin to soften. Mix in the garlic and brown for one minute. Add the spinach and allow to wilt another minute. Push the vegetables to the side and add the chicken back into the inner pot. Use your spatula to scoop most of the vegetables to the top of the chicken.
3. Pour the artichokes and tomatoes onto of the other vegetables and give a gentle stir to mix. Season with salt and pepper and close the lid securely.
4. Rotate the handle to lock the lid and position the steam handle properly to sealing position. Press the poultry button and set the cooking time to 10 minutes.
5. When the Instant Pot® has completed the cooking process release the pressure and allow the float valve to drop. Once it has dropped, remove the lid carefully. Check seasonings and add more if desired. Transfer onto plates and serve immediately.

Ingredients:

- 2 pounds chicken thighs
- 1 tbsp. olive oil, plus 1 tsp
- 1 can artichoke hearts, drained and chopped
- 1 onion, chopped in large pieces
- 1 carrot cut in chunks
- 2 tsp minced garlic
- 3/4 cup grape tomatoes
- 4 cups fresh spinach
- 1/2 cup chicken stock, plus 1 tbsp
- salt, pepper and garlic powder to taste

Preparation time: 15 minutes
Cooking time: 10 minutes
Serves: 4-6

SMOKED PAPRIKA MARINATED CHICKEN

I think paprika may be one of my favorite spices. It's so simple yet so versatile. You can combine it with number of other spices and is always complimentary. But in this dish, oh! It's the star of the show and packs amazing flavors. Of course, any meat cooked in honey, soy sauce and oyster sauce is sure to be pleasing.

Directions:

1. Combine together all marinade ingredients in a large bowl and mix until well incorporated. Add the chicken and coat evenly with the marinade mixture. Chill the chicken for at least 6 hours and remove from the refrigerator 30 minutes before starting the cooking procedure.
2. Place the chicken in the inner pot and pour in the marinade. Close the lid securely and rotate the handle clockwise to lock the lid. Position the steam handle to sealing position, press the poultry button and set the cooking time to 15 minutes.
3. When your Instant Pot® has completed the cooking process, let the pressure release naturally until the float valve drops down. Open the lid, turn the chicken and let it stand for 10 minutes to further cook with low heat. Close the lid.
4. Open the lid, remove the chicken and transfer to a plate and pour the sauce over top. Serve immediately.

Ingredients:

- 1 whole fresh chicken, cut into 8 portions (or substitute a mixture of boneless, skinless breasts and thighs, approximately 1 1/2 pounds of chicken)

Marinade

- 1 tablespoon of smoked paprika
- 1 teaspoon table salt
- 2 tablespoons of raw honey
- 1 tablespoon of tamari soy sauce
- 1 tablespoon of oyster sauce
- ½ teaspoon coarsely ground black pepper
- 1 teaspoon minced garlic
- ½ cup chicken stock

Preparation time: 10 minutes (6 hours to marinade)
Cooking time: 25 minutes
Serves: 6 to 8

NEW ORLEANS STYLE BARBECUE SHRIMP

On Christmas Eve, our family always serves a bunch of appetizer dishes for dinner and we always prepare this. It can be served as a meal or an appetizer. This sauce is quite tasty and the Instant Pot® never fails to cook the shrimp perfectly.

Directions:

1. Combine together all sauce ingredients in a bowl and mix until well incorporated. Lightly grease the inner pot and add the sauce ingredients. Press the sauté button and bring the mixture to a boil.
2. Add the shrimp and gently toss to evenly coat the shrimp with the sauce. Close the lid securely and rotate the handle clockwise the lock the lid. Position the steam vent to sealing position, press the manual button and set the cooking time to 15 minutes.
3. When the pressure cooker has finished the cooking cycle, release the pressure naturally until the float valve drops down. Let it stand for 5 minutes to further cook with low heat.
4. Open the lid, remove and discard the thyme and briefly stir to coat the shrimp.
5. Transfer to a serving platter and serve immediately with lemon wedges.

Ingredients:

- 2 pounds of fresh medium-sized shrimps, peeled and deveined
- 1 lemon, cut into wedges
- 1 teaspoon of cooking oil

For the Sauce

- ½ cup of unsalted butter
- 3 tablespoons of Worcestershire sauce
- juice of 2 lemons
- 2 tablespoons white wine
- ¼ cup chicken stock
- 2 tablespoons chili sauce
- ½ tablespoon coarsely ground black pepper
- 2 teaspoons seafood seasoning mix (such as Old Bay)
- ½ tablespoon of smoked paprika
- ½ teaspoon of table salt
- 3 garlic cloves, chopped
- 1 sprig of fresh thyme

Preparation time: 10 minutes Cooking time: 25 minutes Serves: 4 to 6

CITRUS PRAWN & PEA RISOTTO

This is an appealing, simple meal that is light but still filling. I like to serve it as a special lunch along with a citrus fruit salad.

Directions:

1. Heat the oil in the inner pot of the pressure cooker, press sauté and add the shrimp. Cook the shrimp for 4 minutes or until it turns opaque in color and remove from the inner pot. Set aside and add the onions to the inner pot. Sauté the onions for 5 minutes or until soft and tender, and then stir in the rice. Sauté for 5 minutes until the rice is evenly coated with oil.
2. Pour in the wine, cook until the liquid has reduced in half and then add the stock. Return the shrimp to the inner pot and stir in the crushed red pepper flakes, lemon juice and peas. Season to taste with salt and pepper and stir to combine.
3. Close the lid securely and rotate the handle clockwise to lock the lid. Position the steam handle properly to sealing position, press the porridge button and set the cooking to 5 minutes.
4. When your Instant Pot® has completed the cooking cycle, let the pressure release naturally. Do not use the quick release method in releasing the pressure.
5. Portion onto individual serving plates and serve with grated lemon zest on top.

Ingredients:

- 2 tablespoons of cooking oil
- 1 medium onion, diced
- 1 cup of risotto rice, rinsed and drained
- ½ cup of white wine
- 2 cups of fish stock or vegetable stock
- 1 pound of fresh shrimp, peeled and deveined
- Salt and black pepper, to taste
- 1 cup of peas
- 1 teaspoon of crushed red pepper flakes
- 1 lemon, juiced and zested

Preparation time: 5 minutes
Cooking time: 25 minutes
Serves: 4

SHRIMP SCAMPI

This scampi dish can be made in mere minutes. I like to peel the shrimp before serving and then mix it back in with the rice, topping with a little more melted butter and then a quick sprinkle of cheese.

Directions:

1. Add the butter to the inner pot and press the sauté button. Allow butter to melt, then add minced garlic. Allow butter and garlic to cook for one minute. Press cancel/ keep warm button.
2. Add remaining ingredients, except shrimp and give a quick stir to mix. Add shrimp to the top of the rice mixture.
3. Close the lid securely and rotate the handle clockwise to lock the lid. Position the steam release handle to sealing position, press the manual button and set the cooking time to 5 minutes.
4. When the pressure cooker has completed the cooking cycle, quick release the pressure cooker and open the lid when the float valve drops down. Remove shrimp and rice to a serving bowl.
5. Shrimp can be served as peel-and-eat or go ahead and peel before stirring back into the rice mixture.
6. This dish can be served with garnishes of melted butter, lemon juice or parmesan cheese.

Ingredients:

- 1 pound frozen shrimp, 16-20 count with tails and shells still on
- 1/4 cup butter
- 1 cup Jasmine rice
- 1/4 cup parsley
- 1 teaspoon salt
- 1/4 teaspoon pepper
- 1 lemon, juiced
- 1 1/2 cups chicken broth
- 1 tbsp. minced garlic

Preparation time: 5 minutes
Cooking time: 5 minutes
Serves: 3-4

CALAMARI IN TOMATO SAUCE

If you enjoy calamari then this recipe is a clear winner. The sauce is aromatic and full of flavor. Using the Instant Pot® takes all the guess work out of whether or not the calamari is cooked. This is excellent over pasta.

Directions:

1. Add the oil into the inner pot of your Instant Pot®, press the sauté button and cook the garlic, red pepper flakes and anchovies for 4 minutes while stirring regularly. Stir in the squid rings and sauté for 4 minutes while stirring regularly to evenly coat the squid with oil. Pour in the wine and cook until it has reduced in half. Add the stock, tomatoes and half of the parsley into the inner pot and stir to combine.
2. Close the lid securely and rotate the handle to lock the lid. Position the steam release handle to sealing position, press the manual button and set the cooking time to 15 minutes.
3. When the pressure cooker has completed the cooking cycle, let the pressure release naturally until the float valve drops down. Open the lid and stir in the lemon juice and remaining parsley and season to taste with salt and pepper. Let it stand for 10 minutes in keep warm mode to further cook with low heat.
4. Transfer to a serving platter and serve immediately.

Ingredients:

- 1 ½ pounds of fresh squid or calamari, heads removed and body sliced into rounds
- 1 ½ cup of stewed tomatoes
- ½ cup of dry white wine
- 1 cup fish stock
- 2 garlic cloves, crushed
- ½ cup loosely packed fresh parsley leaves, chopped
- 2 anchovies, chopped
- ½ teaspoon of crushed red pepper flakes
- juice from 1 lemon
- 2 tablespoons of oil
- Salt and black pepper, to taste

Preparation time: 15 minutes
Cooking time: 35 minutes
Serves: 4 to 6

TILAPIA WITH ORANGE-GINGER SAUCE

Tilapia is an easy fish to prepare and enjoy. This citrus-ginger sauce packs so much flavor and really takes this dish to the next level. Steaming is a healthy and simple way to enjoy tilapia and it's so easy to do in the Instant Pot®. Be sure to coat the steam rack with a bit of cooking spray so the fish doesn't stick.

Directions:

1. Pat-dry the fish with paper towels and lightly brush with oil on both sides. Season both sides with salt and pepper and set aside.
2. Add the orange zest, orange juice, ginger, spring onions, white wine and stock in the inner pot and place the steam rack over the mixture. Place the fish on the steam rack and close the lid securely.
3. Rotate the handle clockwise to lock the lid and position the steam release handle to sealing position. Press the steam button and set the time to 7 minutes.
4. When your Instant Pot® has completed the cooking cycle, let the pressure release naturally until the float valve drops down. Transfer to a plate and serve with sauce. If the sauce is not yet thick, cook further until the desired consistency is achieved.

Ingredients:

- 4 fresh tilapia fish fillets
- 1 orange, juiced and zested
- 1-inch piece of fresh ginger roots, minced
- 3 stems of spring onions, chopped or sliced
- 1 tablespoon of cooking oil
- Salt and black pepper, to taste
- ½ cup of dry white wine
- ½ cup of fish stock

Preparation time: 5 minutes
Cooking time: 15 to 20 minutes
Serves: 4

COCONUT FISH CURRY

A creamy dish, with just a bit of spice this curry is easy enough for a weekday meal but impressive enough to serve to guests. Use your favorite fish and adjust the spiciness by adding more or less jalapeno.

Directions:

1. Add the oil into the inner pot of the pressure cooker, press the sauté button and fry the bay and kaffir lime leaves until lightly brown. Stir in the onion, garlic, and ginger and sauté until soft and fragrant. Stir in the cumin, turmeric, red pepper flakes and curry paste and cook for 5 minutes or until aromatic.
2. Add the coconut milk and bring it to a boil while scraping the browned bits on the bottom of the pot. Stir in the tomato, jalapeno and the fish and stir to combine. Season with salt and white pepper and close the lid securely.
3. Rotate the handle to lock the lid and position the steam release handle to sealing position. Press the soup button and set the cooking time to 7 minutes.
4. When the pressure cooker has completed the cooking cycle, let the pressure release naturally until the float valve drops down. Open the lid, discard the leaves and stir in the lemon juice.
5. Transfer to a serving bowl and serve warm.

Ingredients:

- 1 ½ pound of fresh tuna steaks or any fish fillets, cut into bite-size pieces
- 1 tablespoon of oil
- 1 large ripe red tomato, diced
- 2 jalapeno peppers, sliced
- 1 large white onion, halved and thinly sliced
- 2 crushed garlic cloves
- 1-inch piece of fresh ginger root, grated
- 3 bay leaves
- 3 kaffir lime leaves
- ½ tablespoon of cumin powder
- ½ teaspoon turmeric powder
- 1 teaspoon crushed red pepper flakes
- 1 tablespoon of green curry paste
- 2 cups of coconut cream or milk
- 1 teaspoon of salt
- ¼ teaspoon ground white pepper
- juice from 1/2 a lemon

Preparation time: 5 minutes
Cooking time: 30 minutes
Serves:

SHRIMP ETOUFFEE

When my husband and I were dating our favorite place to go to dinner was a restaurant owned by a transplanted Louisiana chef. The food was so authentic and my husband always ordered the shrimp étouffée. Unfortunately we don't live anywhere near that restaurant anymore and we are hours from the Gulf, but this recipe always satisfies when my husband has a craving for this shrimp dish.

Directions:

1. Add the butter in the inner pot of the pressure cooker, press sauté and melt the butter. Gradually add the flour and Cajun seasoning and cook until lightly brown while stirring regularly. Add the onions, garlic, sweet pepper, celery and the salt to the inner pot and cook for 5 minutes or until the vegetables are soft and aromatic.
2. Pour in the stock, bring to a boil and stir while scraping the bottom of the pot. Add the tomatoes and close the lid securely.
3. Rotate the handle clockwise to lock the lid and position the steam release handle properly to sealing position. Press the manual button and set the cooking time to 10 minutes. When your Instant Pot® has completed the cooking cycle, let the pressure release naturally until the float valve drops down.
4. Season the shrimp with Cajun spice rub and salt and toss to evenly coat the shrimp with the seasonings. Open the lid and place the shrimp in the inner pot. Close and lock the lid and cook for about 5 minutes or until it returns to a simmer. Remove the shrimp, transfer to a serving bowl and adjust the seasoning according to preferred taste.
5. Pour the soup into the bowl with the shrimp, and serve immediately with chopped parsley on top.

Ingredients:

- 2 pounds of fresh small shrimp, peeled and deveined
- 1 tablespoon Cajun spice rub (for seasoning shrimp)
- ½ teaspoon kosher salt
- 1/4 cup minced parsley
- salt and pepper to taste
- 4 cups fish or shrimp stock
- ¼ cup of butter
- 3 tablespoon of sifted flour
- ½ tablespoon of Cajun spice rub
- 1 cup of minced white onion
- 1 medium stalk of celery, finely chopped
- 1 green sweet pepper, finely chopped
- 4 garlic cloves, minced
- ½ teaspoon of salt
- 2 cups of canned tomatoes, diced
- Chopped parsley, for serving

Preparation time: **20 minutes**
Cooking time: **25 minutes**
Serves:

LOBSTER TAILS

On our first Christmas as a married couple, my husband and I weren't able to travel to be with family on Christmas Day. We used this as an excuse to treat ourselves to lobster tails dripping in a garlicky butter sauce. It is still one of our most memorable Christmases, just a simple time of being together. I didn't have an Instant Pot® back then, but have made this recipe more recently and it is an excellent, easy way to prepare flawless lobster tails.

Directions:

1. Add the water in the inner pot and place the steam rack in the pressure cooker. Place the lobster tail skin side down on the steam rack and season with salt and pepper.
2. Close the lid securely and rotate the handle clockwise to lock the lid. Position the steam release handle to sealing position, press the steam button and set the cooking time to 5 minutes. When the Instant Pot® has completed the cooking cycle, use the quick release method in releasing the pressure and open the lid.
3. Remove the lobster from the pressure cooker and transfer to a plate. Drizzle with clarified butter and sprinkle lightly with salt, serve warm with lemon wedges if desired.

Ingredients:

- 1 cup of water
- 1 pound of lobster tails, cut across the middle into halves
- 2 tablespoons of clarified butter
- Salt and ground black pepper, to taste
- Lemon wedges, for serving (optional)

Preparation time: 5 minutes
Cooking time: 10 minutes
Serves: 3 to 4

COD WITH PEAS IN PESTO SAUCE

Cod is a pretty appealing fish to eat even for people that don't just LOVE fish. It's a simple white fish that is mild in flavor and therefore making it an excellent choice to serve with a creamy sauce. The chopped almonds really do add a lot of crunch and fun to this dish so don't leave them out, unless you just must!

Directions:

1. Add all ingredients for the almond pesto in a food processor and pulse into a coarse mixture. Add the wine and pulse to combine and transfer to a bowl and set aside.
2. Place your steam rack in the inner pot of the pressure cooker and set fish on the rack. Season with salt and pepper. Pour in 1 cup of water to the bottom of the inner pot. Close the lid securely and rotate the handle clockwise to lock the lid. Position the steam release handle to sealing position, press the steam button and set the time to 4 minutes.
3. When the Instant Pot® has completed the cooking cycle, quick release the pressure cooker and open the lid when the float valve drops down. Remove the fish and add the peas into the inner pot, let the peas stand for at least 5 minutes or until heated through. Drain any access water before serving the peas.
4. Place the fish on a serving platter and top with the peas. Drizzle over half of the pesto sauce on the fish and serve with chopped almonds on top. Serve extra pesto on the side. (Pesto can be warmed before serving using your preferred method, such as stovetop or microwave. It can also be served room temperature.)

Ingredients:

- 1 pound of fresh cod fillets, each fillet sliced into 4 equal portions
- 1 cup of canned peas
- 1 cup of white wine
- 2 tablespoons of chopped almonds
- Salt and black pepper, to taste

For the Almond pesto

- ½ cup loosely packed fresh parsley leaves
- 2 tablespoons of chopped almonds
- 2 crushed garlic cloves
- 1 teaspoon of dried oregano leaves
- 1 teaspoon of smoked paprika

Preparation time: 20 minutes
Cooking time: 15 minutes
Serves: 6

SALMON IN WHITE WINE

You probably know that salmon is a healthy choice, but did you know why? Salmon is loaded with vitamin B-12 and vitamin D and is rich in Omega 3- fatty acids. In other words, it is a great health conscience choice to eat salmon at least once a week. Here is a great way to prepare it in your Instant Pot®.

Directions:

1. Place the onions on the steam rack and add the fish on top of the onions. Transfer the steam rack to the inner pot of the pressure cooker and pour the wine over the fish. Season fish with salt and black pepper and place the lemon wedges on top of the fish.
2. Close and lock the lid securely and position the steam release handle to sealing position. Press the manual button and set the cooking time to 6 minutes.
3. When the Instant Pot® has completed the cooking cycle, use the quick release method in releasing the pressure until the float drops down before opening the lid.
4. Remove the lemon wedges and discard, remove the fish and transfer to a serving platter. Remove the onions and place half of them over the fish and serve immediately.

Ingredients:

- 4 fresh salmon fish fillets
- 1 medium white onion, core removed and sliced into rings
- 3 tablespoons of dry white wine
- Table salt and ground white pepper, to taste
- 1 lemon, slice into wedges

Preparation time: **5 minutes**
Cooking time: **10 minutes**
Serves: **4**

MUSTARD SALMON

I really think that adding the mustard to the salmon adds such a delightful zing to the fish that it makes this one of my favorite ways to prepare it. This is an easy recipe that yields perfectly prepared fish every time.

Directions:

1. Coat the fillets evenly with mustard on both sides and sprinkle with dried thyme leaves on the top side. Place on the steam rack and set aside.
2. Add the wine, stock and bay leaf in the inner pot of the pressure cooker, place the steam rack with the fish in the pressure cooker and close the lid securely.
3. Lock the lid securely and position the steam release handle to sealing position. Press the manual button and set the cooking time to 5 minutes. When the Instant Pot® has completed the cooking cycle, use the quick release method in releasing the pressure until the float valve drops down.
4. Open the lid, remove the fish and transfer to a serving platter. Season with salt and pepper if desired and serve immediately.

Ingredients:

- 4 fresh salmon fish fillets
- 1 tablespoons of yellow or Dijon mustard
- 1 teaspoon dried thyme leaves
- ½ cup of white wine
- ½ cup of fish stock
- 1 bay leaf
- Salt and pepper, to taste (optional)

Preparation time: 5 minutes
Cooking time: 10 minutes
Serves: 2 to 4

LOW COUNTRY SHRIMP BOIL

Every year when we go to the beach we do a big shrimp boil, complete with newspaper all over the table and big bowls for all the shells and corn husk leftovers. This is a great way to get a bit of that taste of the sea without actually having to be there. Be sure to spread some newspaper on your table, too. It adds to the authenticity of it and sure makes for easy cleaning!

Directions:

1. In the inner pot of the pressure cooker, add the oil and press the sauté button. Add the chicken, season to taste with salt and pepper and cook until evenly browned on both sides. Remove from the pressure cooker, transfer to a plate and add the shrimp into the inner pot. Cook until opaque while stirring occasionally and transfer to a separate plate. Set aside.
2. Mix together the lemon juice, crab boil seasoning, butter, bay leaves and wine. Pour into the pot. Layer the chicken evenly on the bottom of the inner pot. Insert the potatoes on the spaces between the chicken pieces. Salt and pepper the potatoes. Layer the corn, shrimp and sausage on top.
3. Close the lid completely and position steam release handle to sealing position.
4. Press the manual button and set the pressure cooking time to 4 minutes.
5. When the pressure cooking cycle is completed, use the natural release method to fully release the pressure. Open the lid when the float valve has dropped down.
6. Adjust seasonings if desired and serve immediately.

Ingredients:

- 4-6 chicken legs
- 1 tablespoon olive oil
- 2 pounds red potatoes, peeled and quartered
- 4-6 links of Andouille sausage
- 2-3 husks of corn, husks and silks removed and cut into thirds
- 1/2 pound of peeled, deveined fresh shrimp
- 2-3 tablespoons of crab boil seasoning
- 1 lemon, juiced
- salt and pepper, to taste
- 2-3 tablespoons of dry white wine
- 2 tablespoons of unsalted butter
- 2 bay leaves

Preparation time: 10 minutes
Cooking time: 25-30 minutes
Serves: 4-6

SALMON AND VEGGIES

This is a very simple, yet extremely healthy meal all prepared in one pot. Salmon, carrots and broccoli all steamed in an aromatic broth. The cinnamon and cloves really add an interesting hint of flavor to both the fish and the vegetables.

Directions:

1. Lightly brush the steam rack with oil and lightly coat the fillets on both sides. Place the salmon on the steam rack and set aside.
2. Add the stock, bay leaf, cinnamon and cloves in the inner pot and place the steam rack with fish in the Instant Pot®. Add the vegetables on the sides of the fish and arrange them properly. Close and lock the lid securely and then position the steam release handle to sealing position. Press the steam button and set the cooking time to 6 minutes.
3. When the pressure cooker has completed the cooking cycle, use the quick release method in releasing the pressure and open the lid when the float valve has dropped down.
4. Remove the steam rack carefully with a cloth and transfer the vegetables and fish to a serving platter with fish on one side and vegetables on the other.
5. Drizzle with cooking sauce and serve immediately.

Ingredients:

- 1 cup vegetable stock
- 1 bay leaf
- 1-inch stick of cinnamon
- 2 to 3 whole cloves
- 2 fresh skin-on salmon fillet
- Oil, to coat salmon and steam rack
- 2 cup of detached broccoli florets
- ½ pound of baby carrots

Preparation time: 10 minutes
Cooking time: 10 minutes
Serves: 2

Rice and Pasta

BROWN RICE

We eat a lot of rice in my family. It's a staple for so many dishes and is a healthy option. And buying rice in bulk saves our family so much money. Using chicken stock and the bouillon base adds great flavor.

Directions:

1. Lightly coat the inner pot of the pressure cooker with oil and add the stock, bouillon base, butter, salt and pepper and stir to combine. Add the rice and stir to distribute evenly with other ingredients and close the lid securely.
2. Rotate the handle clockwise to lock the lid and position the steam release handle to sealing position. Press the rice button and set the cooking time to 12 minutes. When the pressure cooker has completed the cooking cycle, use the quick release method in releasing the pressure and wait until the float valve has dropped down. Let it stand in the Instant Pot® and fluff it before serving.

Ingredients:

- 4 cups of chicken stock
- 1 teaspoon of oil
- 2 cups of long-grain brown rice, rinsed and drained
- 2 tablespoon of chicken bouillon base
- 2 tablespoons of butter
- ½ teaspoon of salt
- ½ teaspoon of black pepper

Preparation time: 5 minutes
Cooking time: 15 minutes
Serves: 4 to 6

ONE POT SPAGHETTI

Easy, one pot spaghetti? Yes, please! This sauce tastes better than jarred, store bought sauce and the pressure cooker cooks the noodles fast. You can have dinner on the table before the troops get too antsy. And did I mention it's all prepared in one pot?

Directions:

1. Add the oil into the inner pot of the pressure cooker, press the sauté button and add the onions, garlic and beef. Sauté until lightly brown and drain excess oil if desired. Stir in the remaining ingredients except for the cheese and pasta and bring to a boil. Add the pasta and toss to coat evenly with the sauce. Break dry noodles in half if they are too big to fit in pot.
2. Close and lock the lid securely and position the steam vent to sealing position. Press the manual button and set the cooking time to 6 minutes.
3. When the Instant Pot® has completed the cooking cycle, use the quick release method in releasing the pressure until the float valve drops down.
4. Open the lid, portion pasta and sauce into individual serving plates and serve immediately with grated Parmesan on top.

Ingredients:

- 2 tablespoons of cooking oil
- 1 pound of ground beef
- 1 large white onion, diced
- 1 teaspoon minced garlic
- 2 cup of canned tomato sauce
- 1 cup of red wine
- 1 cup beef stock
- 1 pound of spaghetti pasta (uncooked)
- ½ tablespoon of ground chili powder
- 1 ½ teaspoon of salt
- ¼ cup of Parmesan cheese, grated

Preparation time: **5 minutes**
Cooking time: **15 minutes**
Serves: **6**

BOLOGNESE RAGU PASTA SAUCE

By now you have probably realized that if a recipe has bacon or heavy cream it's probably at the top of my list. And this particular recipe has both! This is a simple quick recipe to prepare that can probably be made with things you already have in your kitchen. I've found it to be very kid and picky eater friendly, too.

Directions:

1. Add the bacon in the inner pot and press the sauté button to cook the bacon. When the bacon has released its oil, add the onions, celery and carrots and sauté until soft and tender. Stir in the ground beef and sauté until lightly browned and most of the liquid has evaporated. Pour in the wine and cook while scraping the browned bits from the bottom of the pot until it the liquid has reduced in half.
2. Combine 1 cup of beef stock, tomato paste, salt and pepper in a mixing bowl and mix until well combined. Pour into the inner pot and stir just to combine. Close and lock the lid securely and position the steam release handle to sealing position. Press the manual button and set the cooking time to 10 minutes.
3. When the pressure cooker has completed the cooking cycle, use the quick release method in releasing the pressure until the float valve drops down. Open the lid and stir in the remaining stock with the pasta, cook further until it returns to a boil and press the cancel button to stop cooking.
4. Keep it warm in the Instant Pot® and stir in the cream just before it is served.

Ingredients:

- ½ cup of chopped bacon
- 1 white onion, diced
- 2 cups cooked spaghetti pasta
- ½ cup of diced carrot
- ½ cup of chopped celery
- ½ pound of ground beef
- 3 tablespoon of dry red wine
- ¼ cup of tomato paste
- 2 cups of brown beef stock (divided)
- 1 to ½ teaspoon of salt
- ½ teaspoon ground black pepper
- 2 tablespoons of heavy cream

Preparation time: 10 minutes
Cooking time: 45 minutes
Serves: 4 to 6

RISOTTO

Risotto can be very scary to someone who is new to the kitchen or doesn't have experience with this particular dish. So much stirring! But with the pressure cooker, anyone can achieve a perfect, tasty risotto. Only normal amounts of stirring required.

Directions:

1. Add the oil to the inner pot, press the sauté button and sauté the onions for 3 minutes or until soft and tender. Stir in the rice and toss to coat evenly with oil. Cook for 5 minutes or until the rice is lightly toasted. Deglaze with wine and cook until the wine has reduced while scraping the bottom of the pan. Add the stock, season to taste with salt and pepper and briefly stir to combine.
2. Close and lock the lid securely and position the steam release handle to sealing position. Press the rice button and set the cooking time to 10 minutes.
3. When the Instant Pot® has completed the cooking cycle, use the quick release method in releasing the pressure until the float valve has dropped down. Remove the lid and fluff the rice.
4. Transfer to a serving platter or bowl and serve warm with grated Parmesan on top.

Ingredients:

- 2 cups short-grain white rice or Arborio Rice, rinsed and drained
- 4 cups of chicken stock
- 1 medium white onion, diced
- 1-2 tablespoons of white wine
- 1 tablespoon of oil
- 2 tablespoons of grated Parmesan cheese
- salt and ground black pepper, to taste

Preparation time: 5 minutes
Cooking time: 20 minutes
Serves: 4 to 6

SPANISH RICE

This is not your standard Spanish rice. It is so much better. First of all, it can pretty much be a meal itself, so that's a bonus. Second, the flavors that develop as the rice cooks in the tomato sauce and beef broth is going to make your mouth so happy. And last but certainly not least, it is topped with cheesy goodness! And black olives, if you are an olive lover. So make this dish soon!

Directions:

1. Add the oil into the inner pot of the pressure cooker, press the sauté button and add the garlic, onions and sweet pepper. Sauté for 4 minutes or until soft and fragrant and stir in the ground beef. Cook until the beef is lightly browned or for about 10 minutes while stirring regularly.
2. Stir in the rice and cook for 2 minutes until evenly coated with beef mixture while stirring occasionally.
3. Add in the tomato sauce, beef stock, salt and pepper and close the lid securely. Rotate the handle clockwise to lock the lid and position the steam release handle to sealing position. Press the manual button and set the cooking time to 6 minutes.
4. When the pressure cooker has completed the cooking cycle, use the quick release method in releasing the pressure until the float valve drops down.
5. Open the lid and check to see if the rice is done. If it is not yet done, cook further with low heat until the desired texture is achieved. Keep it warm in the pressure cooker before serving. Top with cheese and black olives.

Ingredients:

- 2 tablespoons of oil
- 1 cup of diced onion
- ½ teaspoon of minced garlic
- 1 medium green sweet pepper, diced
- 1 pound of ground beef
- 2 cups of long-grain white rice, rinsed and drained
- 3 cups of canned tomato sauce
- 1 ½ cups of beef stock
- 1 teaspoon of salt
- ½ teaspoon of ground black pepper
- 1 cup of Cheddar cheese, shredded
- ½ cup of black olives

Preparation time: 10 minutes
Cooking time: 25 minutes
Serves: 6 to 8

CHICKEN ENCHILADA PASTA

This is an easy weeknight dish that everyone is sure to love. It features pasta, chicken, and cheese all mixed in a flavorful, sauce. The pasta even cooks in the pressure cooker saving you time and one less dish to wash!

Directions:

1. Add the oil into the inner cooking pot, press the sauté button and add the onions when the oil is hot. Sauté for 3 minutes or until the onions are soft and stir in the garlic. Add in the enchilada sauce, stock, tomatoes and taco seasoning in the inner pot and stir to combine. Sauté one minute for flavors to develop.
2. Add the chicken and pasta, briefly stir and close the lid securely. Rotate the handle clockwise to lock the lid and position the steam release handle to sealing position. Press the manual button and set the cooking time to 5 minutes.
3. When the pressure cooker has completed the cooking cycle, use the quick release method in releasing the steam until the float valve drops down. Open the lid and briefly stir to distribute the ingredients evenly, transfer to a baking dish and top with shredded cheese before serving. If desired, garnish with optional ingredients listed above.

Ingredients:

- 1 tablespoon of cooking oil
- 1 medium white onion, diced
- 2 cloves garlic, diced
- 2 cups of enchilada sauce
- 1 cup canned roasted tomatoes
- 1 cup of chicken stock
- 1 tablespoon of taco seasoning mix
- 2 fresh chicken breasts fillets, cut into cubes
- 1 pound of rotini pasta (uncooked)
- 2 cups of Cheddar cheese, shredded

For garnish (optional)
- Green onions
- Olives
- Diced tomatoes
- Cilantro

Preparation time: 10 minutes
Cooking time: 15 minutes
Serves: 6

MAC AND CHEESE

I don't know about you, but mac and cheese is pretty much a staple at my house. And it's not just about the kiddos. My husband and I both love the creamy, comforting noodles. But we have become slight mac and cheese snobs and really all of us prefer the homemade version. Here is a super easy recipe that can be dumped in the pressure cooker and cooks in about 5 minutes. Even easier than the blue box and so much tastier!

Directions:

1. Combine the milk, cornstarch, onion powder, salt, black pepper and mustard powder in the inner pot and mix to combine. Add the remaining ingredients and stir until well incorporated.
2. Close and lock the lid securely and position the steam release handle to sealing position. Press the manual button and set the cooking time to 5 minutes. Use the quick release method in releasing the pressure until the float valve has dropped down. Open the lid and stir until the ingredients are evenly distributed and the cheese has melted.
3. Let it stand in the pressure cooker in keep warm mode until the cheese has completely melted before serving. Or press the sauté button and cook just to melt the cheese.

Ingredients:

- 3 cups of chicken stock
- 1 1/2 pounds of cooked elbow macaroni
- 1 ½ cup of evaporated milk
- 2 tablespoon of cornstarch
- 1 teaspoon of salt
- ½ teaspoon of ground black pepper
- ½ tablespoon of onion powder
- ½ tablespoon of dry mustard powder
- 3 to 4 cups of shredded cheddar cheese
- 1 cup of Parmesan cheese, grated
- 2 tablespoons of butter
- ½ cup of cream cheese

Preparation time: 10 minutes
Cooking time: 15 minutes
Serves: 6 to 8

CHICKEN ALFREDO

This classic dish is great when you have leftover chicken and are looking for something special to do with it. Using jarred Alfredo sauce means that this dish can be ready and on the table in a very short time. Pressure cooking all of the ingredients together makes magic happen in the pot. The flavors all meld together making this a savory meal.

Directions:

1. Add the oil into the inner cooking pot of the pressure cooker, press the sauté button and add the chicken when the oil is hot. Sauté for 3 minutes or until lightly browned and add in the bouillon base, Alfredo sauce, garlic, black pepper and egg noodles into the inner pot and stir to combine.
2. Close and lock the lid securely, position the steam release handle to sealing position and press the manual button. Set the cooking time to 5 minutes.
3. When the pressure cooker has completed the cooking cycle, use the quick release method in releasing the pressure until the float valve drops down.
4. Open the lid and transfer the pasta to a serving platter and serve with grated parmesan on top.

Ingredients:

- 1 tablespoon of oil
- ½ pound of egg noodles, cooked ahead
- 2 cups of Alfredo sauce in jar
- 1 cup of diced precooked chicken
- 1 tablespoon of chicken bouillon base
- 1 tablespoon of chopped roasted garlic
- ½ teaspoon of crushed black pepper
- Grated Parmesan cheese, for garnish (optional)

Preparation time: 8 minutes
Cooking time: 12 minutes
Serves: 3 to 4

ZITI WITH SAUSAGE

This is a fun, easy meal that can be great for weeknights, but also substantial enough to serve to guests. Sweet Italian sausage is a favorite of mine. I also like to sprinkle a little parmesan cheese on top right before serving. Pair with some garlic bread and a salad and dinner is done!

Directions:

1. Add the oil into the inner cooking pot and press the sauté button. Once the oil is hot, add the sausage, onions and bell pepper and cook for 5 minutes or until sausage is no longer pink. Add the tomato sauce and stock and bring to a boil. Stir in the pasta and close the lid.
2. Rotate the handle clockwise to lock the lid and position the steam vent to sealing position. Press the manual button and set the cooking time to 5 minutes.
3. When the Instant Pot® has completed the cooking cycle, use the natural release method in releasing the pressure until the float valve drops down.
4. Open the lid, season to taste with salt and pepper and transfer into individual serving bowls. Serve warm with chopped basil leaves in top.

Ingredients:

- 1 tablespoon of cooking oil
- 4 links of sweet Italian sausage, casings removed and chopped
- 1 medium onion, minced
- 1 medium bell pepper, diced
- 2 cups of canned tomato sauce
- 3 cups of chicken stock
- 3 cups of ziti noodles
- 1/4 cup of chopped fresh basil leaves
- Salt and ground black pepper, to taste

Preparation time: 10 minutes
Cooking time: 15 minutes
Serves: 4 to 6

CHEESY CHICKEN AND BROCCOLI WITH RICE

My kids like broccoli but sometimes it is still chore to get them to eat it. Not with this meal! Another one pot wonder that will frequently grace my table, this one is a crowd pleaser. It's comfort food at its finest while still being healthy for my family.

Directions:

1. Add the oil into the inner cooking pot, press the sauté button. Once the oil is hot, add the onions and chicken and cook for 5 minutes while stirring occasionally. Stir in the rice, stock, salt, black pepper and garlic powder and briefly stir to combine.
2. Close and lock the lid securely and position the steam release handle to sealing position. Pressure cook on high for 5 minutes and use the quick release method in releasing the pressure. When the float valve drops, open the lid and stir in the milk-flour mixture, broccoli and cheese and cook until it returns to a boil and the sauce has thickened.
3. Portion into individual serving plates and serve with grated Parmesan on top.

Ingredients:

- 1 tablespoon of cooking oil
- 1 pound of boneless, skinless chicken breasts, cut into cubes
- 1 medium white onion, chopped
- 1 ½ cups of long-grain white rice, rinsed and drained
- 2 cups of chicken stock
- ½ teaspoon of salt
- ½ teaspoon of ground pepper
- ½ teaspoon of garlic powder
- 2 tablespoons of sifted flour and ½ cup of milk mixture for thickening
- 1 cup of Cheddar cheese, shredded
- 2 cups of detached broccoli florets
- Grated Parmesan, for serving

Preparation time: 15 minutes
Cooking time: 15 minutes
Serves: 4 to 6

CHEESY MEATY PASTA

Really, the name of the recipe says it all. Who doesn't love a little meat and cheese with their pasta? This tastes a bit like a casserole without all the hassle of boiling noodles and sautéing meat and veggies in separate pans. All the prep and the cooking can be done in the pressure cooker.

Directions:

1. Add the ghee to the inner cooking pot of the Instant Pot® press the sauté button and add the onions, garlic, carrots and celery when the ghee is hot. Sauté for 5 minutes or until the vegetables are soft and then add the ground beef. Cook until the meat is lightly browned and season to taste with salt and black pepper.
2. When the liquid has reduced completely, stir in the red wine and cook until it has evaporated fully while scraping the browned bits on the bottom of the pan. Stir in the pasta, pureed tomatoes and add enough stock just to cover all of the ingredients. Briefly stir to combine and close the lid securely.
3. Lock the lid and position the steam release handle to sealing position. Pressure cook on high for 5 minutes and use the quick release method in releasing the pressure. When the float valve has dropped down, open the lid and stir the mixture to distribute the ingredients evenly. Let it sit in the Instant Pot® until the pasta is fully cooked and season with salt and black pepper if needed.
4. Transfer the mixture into a serving bowl or portion into individual serving dishes, and then serve immediately with shredded cheese on top.

Ingredients:

- 1 tablespoon of ghee/clarified butter
- ½ cup minced white onion
- ½ cup minced carrot
- ½ cup finely chopped celery stalk
- 2 garlic cloves, minced
- 2 tablespoons of red wine
- 2 cups of red tomato puree
- 1 pound of short pasta, such as penne or rotini
- 1 pound of ground beef
- Beef stock, as needed to cover the meat-pasta mixture
- 1 cup of shredded Mozzarella cheese
- ½ tablespoon of salt
- 1 teaspoon of ground black pepper

Preparation time: 10 minutes
Cooking time: 20 minutes
Serves: 4

LENTILS AND RICE

Lentils and rice are a great combination of healthy and tasty. This meal is as aromatic as it is flavorful. I think cooking all of it in the chicken broth instead of water is preferable because it adds a little more depth to the flavors.

Directions:

1. Add all ingredients in the inner cooking pot of the pressure cooker and briefly stir to combine. Close and lock the lid securely and position the steam release handle to sealing position.
2. Press the rice button and wait until the pressure cooker switches to keep warm mode. Use the natural release method in releasing the pressure fully until the float valve drops down. Open the lid and fluff the rice. Keep it warm in the pressure cooker before serving. Remove cinnamon stick and cloves.
3. Top with minced parsley and drizzle with lemon juice. Serve warm.

Ingredients:

- 1 ½ cup of any brown rice variety, rinsed and drained
- ½ to 1 cup of lentils
- 3 cups of chicken stock
- 1-inch piece of cinnamon stick
- 4 whole cloves
- ½ teaspoon of ground cumin
- ½ teaspoon of black pepper, freshly ground
- Salt, to taste

For serving

- 2 tablespoons of minced fresh parsley leaves, for serving
- ½ lemon, juiced for serving

Preparation time: **10 minutes**
Cooking time: **25 minutes**
Serves: **4**

MEXICAN RED RICE

This Mexican rice is a super side dish to many of the main course entrees in this book. It is more interesting and flavorful than plain white or brown rice.

Directions:

1. Add the clarified butter in the inner cooking pot and press the sauté button. When the butter is hot, sauté the garlic for 3 minutes or until lightly brown and stir in the rice. Sauté for 5 minutes or until the rice is evenly coated with butter and lightly toasted.
2. Stir in the remaining ingredients and stir to combine. Season to taste with salt and black pepper and close the lid securely.
3. Lock the lid and position the steam release handle to sealing position. Press the rice button and cook until the pressure cooker switches to keep warm mode.
4. When the pressure cooker has completed the cooking cycle, release the pressure fully using the quick release method and wait until the float valve has dropped down before opening the lid. Open the lid and fluff the rice before serving.
5. If the rice is not done, cook further in keep warm mode until the rice is fully cooked. Add more stock if needed until desired texture is achieved.
6. Keep it warm in the Instant Pot® before serving.

Ingredients:

- 2 tablespoons of clarified butter
- 2 cups of long-grain or short-grain red rice, rinsed and drained
- 3 cups of chicken or vegetable stock
- 1 cup of canned stewed tomatoes with green chilies
- 4 garlic cloves, crushed and peeled
- 2 tablespoons of tomato paste
- Salt and black pepper

Preparation time: **10 minutes**
Cooking time: **15 minutes**
Serves: **6**

MUSHROOM "RISOTTO"

This is an easy risotto that is sure to impress featuring tiny, cute button mushrooms. Yes, I think button mushrooms are cute. And flavorful! Even if you've never cooked a risotto in your life, this is a simple way to start. The Instant Pot® does all the hard work and you get to take all the credit.

Directions:

1. Add the oil into the inner cooking pot of the pressure cooker and press the sauté button. Once the oil is hot, sauté the mushrooms, shallots and garlic for 3 minutes or until soft and fragrant. Stir in the rice and cook for 3 minutes while stirring to evenly coat the rice with oil. Add 1 cup of stock and cook until the liquid has reduced in half while stirring regularly.
2. Pour in the remaining stock and season to taste with salt and black pepper. Close and lock the lid securely and then position the steam release handle to sealing position. Press the rice button and cook until the pressure cooker switches to keep warm mode.
3. When the pressure cooker switches to keep warm mode, use the natural release method in releasing the pressure until the float valve drops down. Let it stand for 10 minutes before opening the lid to further cook with low heat.
4. Open the lid and fluff the rice. If the rice is not yet fully cooked, add more stock if needed and further cook in keep warm mode until the desired texture is achieved.
5. Keep it warm in the Instant Pot® before serving, and then serve with minced chives and grated Parmesan on top.

Ingredients:

- ½ cup halved button mushrooms
- 2 tablespoons of cooking oil
- ½ cup of minced shallots
- 2 teaspoons of minced garlic cloves
- 1 ½ cups of short-grain rice (Arborio rice)
- 3 cups of chicken stock or vegetable stock
- 1 cup of Parmesan cheese, grated
- Salt and black pepper, as needed to taste
- 2 tablespoons minced chives

Preparation time: 10 minutes
Cooking time: 25 minutes
Serves: 4

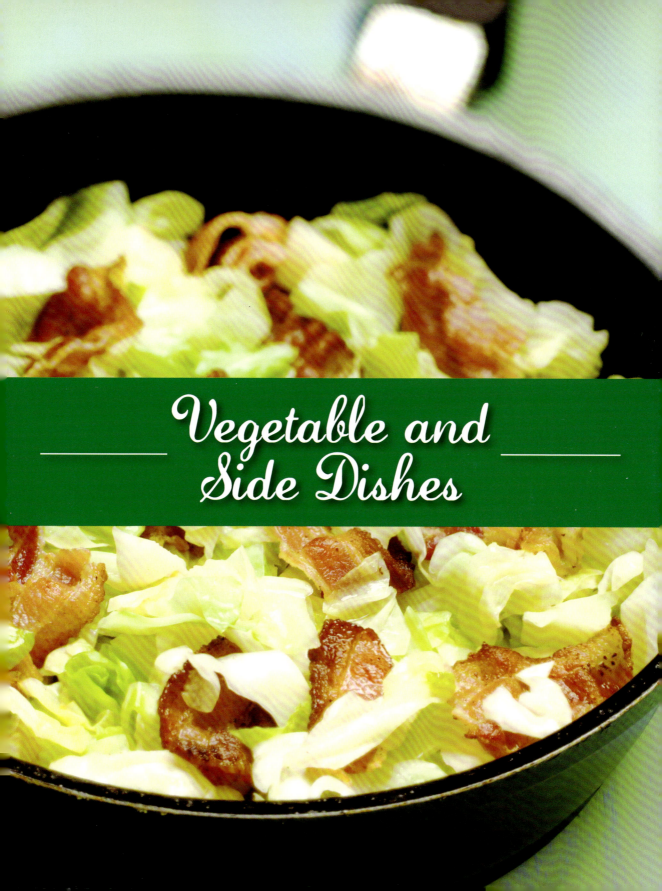

Vegetable and Side Dishes

GREEN BEANS AND BACON

If you've never had pressure cooked green beans then you my friend, are in for a treat! Splurge with the bacon and the sugar, you won't regret it. These might be the tastiest green beans ever.

Directions:

1. Add the bacon and onions into the inner cooking pot of the pressure cooker and press the sauté button to start cooking. Cook the bacon until lightly browned and crispy. Remove bacon and onions from the pot, along with any remaining grease.
2. Add 1 cup of water into the inner cooking pot of the pressure cooker, place the beans in the steam rack and transfer into the pressure cooker. Press steam and set the cooking time to 4 minutes.
3. When the pressure cooker has completed the cooking cycle, use the quick release and open the lid when the float valve drops down. Open the lid, drain the water and add the beans, bacon with the oil, onion and the sugar. Season to taste with salt and pepper and stir to combine. When the sugar has completely dissolved, the beans are ready.
4. Keep the beans warm in the Instant Pot® before serving.

Ingredients:

- 2 pounds of fresh green beans, cut into 2-inch long pieces
- 1/2 cup diced onions
- 1 cup of diced bacon
- 2 tablespoons of sugar
- Salt and black pepper, to taste

Preparation time: 5 minutes
Cooking time: 15 minutes
Serves: 6 to 8

BEER BRAISED CABBAGE WITH BACON

This is not your typical cabbage dish. The bacon and the beer take this to the next level which will have you thinking you aren't eating cabbage at all.

Directions:

1. Add the butter, bacon and oil into the inner cooking pot of the pressure cooker and press the sauté button. Cook for 5 minutes or until the bacon and onions are soft and lightly browned. Pour in the beer and bring to a boil while scraping the browned bits off the bottom of the pot. Add the cabbage, season to taste with salt and pepper and the close the lid securely.
2. Lock the lid and position the steam vent to sealing position. Manually set the cooking time to 3 minutes and cook with high pressure.
3. When the Instant Pot® switches to keep warm mode, quick release the pressure and wait until the float valve drops down.
4. Toss cabbage, adjust seasoning and serve.

Ingredients:

- 1 tablespoon of unsalted butter
- 1 medium white onion, halved and thinly sliced
- ½ cup diced bacon
- 1 medium head of cabbage, core removed and sliced into chiffonade
- ½ cup of light beer
- Salt and black pepper, to taste

Preparation time: 5 minutes
Cooking time: 10 minutes
Serves: 4 to 6

ARTICHOKES

The Instant Pot® makes preparing artichokes simple and fool proof. And it's quick! Serve with your favorite dipping sauce. I like a simple butter lemon sauce.

Directions:

1. Add 2 cups of water, shallots and lemon zest into the inner cooking pot and place the steam rack in the pressure cooker. Place the artichoke heart on the steam rack and season to sprinkle with salt and black pepper.
2. Close and lock the lid securely and position the steam release handle to sealing position. Press steam button and set the cooking time to 6 minutes.
3. When the Instant Pot® has completed the cooking cycle, quick release the pressure and wait until the float valve drops down before opening the lid.
4. Open the lid, remove the artichokes and transfer on a serving platter. Drizzle with lemon juice if desired and serve with dipping sauce.

Ingredients:

- 2 medium hearts of artichoke, halved lengthwise
- 2 cups of water
- 1 lemon, zested
- 2 shallots, minced
- Salt and black pepper, to taste

Preparation time: 5 minutes
Cooking time: 10 minutes
Serves: 2

SICILIAN STUFFED ARTICHOKES

If you are looking for an impressive side dish or appetizer than look no further! The Instant Pot® has this ready in much less time than traditional methods and the tastes are really extraordinary.

Directions:

1. Combine together the croutons, cheese, sweet pepper, onion and anchovies in a large bowl and set aside. In a separate small bowl, combine together the olive oil, oregano, balsamic vinegar and a pinch of salt and pepper.
2. Lightly brush the inner sides of the artichokes with lemon juice and stuff with the crouton mixture. Pack tightly and connect the artichokes back to form into its original figure.
3. Add 1 cup of water into the inner cooking pot, place the artichokes on a steam rack and transfer into the pressure cooker. Close and lock the lid securely and position the steam release handle to sealing position. Press the manual button and set the cooking time to 8 to 10 minutes.
4. When the pressure cooker has completed the cooking cycle, quick release the pressure and wait until the float valve drops down.
5. Open the lid, remove artichokes and transfer to a serving plate. Serve immediately.

Ingredients:

- 1 cup crushed garlic croutons
- 1 small white onion, chopped
- 1 yellow sweet pepper, chopped
- ½ cup of Mozzarella cheese, shredded
- ¼ cup of Parmesan cheese, grated
- 1 tablespoon of finely chopped anchovies
- 2 tablespoons of extra virgin olive oil
- 2 to 3 teaspoons of balsamic vinegar
- 1 teaspoon of dried oregano leaves
- Salt and ground black pepper, to taste
- ¼ cup of chicken stock
- 4 fresh artichokes (large), trimmed and halved lengthwise, center removed
- 1 lemon, juiced
- 1 cup of water

Preparation time: 15 minutes
Cooking time: 15 minutes
Serves: 4

PINTO BEANS

Pinto beans are a staple in many southern kitchens. I do love my Instant Pot® for making it so easy to prepare beans of all varieties. I really do recommend the bacon grease for sautéing the onion, but use whatever you have on hand.

Directions:

1. Add the bacon fat or ghee into the inner cooking pot of the pressure cooker and press the sauté button. Once the oil is hot, sauté the onions for 3 minutes or until soft and translucent. Stir in the remaining ingredients and season with salt to taste. Briefly stir to combine and then close and lock the lid securely.
2. Position the steam release handle to sealing position and pressure cook on high for 40 minutes. When the pressure cooker has completed the cooking cycle, let the pressure release naturally until the float valve drops down.
3. Portion into individual serving dish or bowls and serve immediately.

Ingredients:

- 2 tablespoons of bacon fat or ghee
- 1 medium white onion, diced
- 1 cup loosely packed fresh cilantro leaves and stems, chopped
- 1 teaspoon of ground cumin
- ½ teaspoon of ground chipotle
- 1 pound of raw pinto beans
- 4 cups of vegetable stock
- Salt, as needed to taste

Preparation time: 5 minutes
Cooking time: 40 minutes
Serves: 8

POTATOES AND GREEN BEANS

A quick, easy side dish for a busy lifestyle. The spices really sing in this dish. You might even want to double the recipe to make sure you have leftovers!

Directions:

1. Add the ghee into the inner cooking pot of the pressure cooker and press the sauté button. When the oil is hot, sauté the beans and potatoes for 5 minutes or until evenly coated with oil while stirring regularly. Add all ingredients except for the stock and cook for 1 minute while stirring regularly. Pour in the stock and briefly stir to distribute the ingredients evenly in the inner pot.
2. Close and lock the lid securely and then position the steam release handle sealing position. Press the manual button and pressure cook on high for 7 minutes.
3. When the pressure cooker has completed the cooking cycle, quick release the pressure and wait until the float valve drops down.
4. Open the lid and briefly stir the ingredients, transfer to a serving platter and serve immediately.

Ingredients:

- 1 pound of fresh green beans, cut into 1-inch pieces
- 1 cup of diced potatoes
- 2 cups chicken stock
- 2 tablespoons of ghee
- ½ teaspoon of toasted cumin seeds
- ½ teaspoon of ground turmeric
- Table salt, as needed to taste
- ½ teaspoon of ground cumin
- ½ teaspoon of ground coriander
- ½ teaspoon crushed red pepper flakes
- ½ teaspoon of garam masala spice mix

Preparation time: 5 minutes
Cooking time: 10 minutes
Serves: 4 to 6

ROASTED GARLIC

Roasting garlic will allow you to use the garlic for so many different options. Spread it on pita bread as a dip, use it when making salad dressing, or stir it into creamy mashed potatoes. So many options, you simply must have some of this garlic around! You can even freeze the leftovers.

Directions:

1. Add the water into the inner cooking pot and place the steam rack in the pressure cooker. Add the garlic on the steam rack, close and lock the lid securely.
2. Position the steam release handle to sealing position, set the manual function and set the cooking time to 6 minutes.
3. When the pressure cooker has completed the cooking cycle, quick release the pressure and wait until the float valve drops down. Open the lid, remove the garlic from the inner pot and discard the cooking liquid.
4. Place the garlic in the inner pot and add in the oil to coat the garlic. Push the sauté button, close and cook for about 5 minutes or until the garlic is light browned. Open the lid and remove the garlic.

Ingredients:

- 3 whole heads of garlic, base/core sliced off
- 2 to 3 tablespoons of olive oil
- 1 cup of water

Preparation time: 5 minutes
Cooking time: 15 minutes
Serves: 3 to 4

BEET & CAPER SALAD

I am not a huge beet lover, but have friends who can't get enough of this root vegetable. They are easy to find during the summer at farmers markets and roadside stands. Steaming the beets in the pressure cooker makes preparing this salad a breeze and the dressing is delicious!

Directions:

1. Add all dressing ingredients in a bowl and mix until well combined. Transfer into a jar, close the lid and chill.
2. Add the water into the inner cooking pot and place the steam rack in the pressure cooker. Place the beets on the steam rack and then close and lock the lid securely. Position the steam release handle to sealing position and pressure cook on high for 8 to 10 minutes.
3. When the pressure cooker has completed the cooking cycle, quick release the pressure and wait until the float valve drops down. Open the lid and remove the beets from the inner pot. Let the beets cool completely and peel.
4. Transfer to a serving plate, drizzle with wine vinegar and serve with the dressing mixture.

Ingredients:

- 4 medium-sized fresh beets, trimmed
- 2 tablespoons of rice wine vinegar, for serving
- 1 cup of water

Dressing:

- 2 tablespoons of finely minced fresh parsley leaves
- 1 garlic clove, finely minced
- ½ teaspoon of salt, or as needed to taste
- ¼ teaspoon of ground black pepper
- 2 to 3 teaspoons of olive oil
- 2 tablespoons of canned/jarred capers, chopped

Preparation time: 10 minutes
Cooking time: 15 minutes
Serves: 4

COLLARD GREENS

I first tasted collard greens as a kid and wasn't too impressed but am happy to say that my palate has become more sophisticated since my youth. These collards are a must on any table but especially in the south. They are high in vitamin A and vitamin K as well, making them a healthy side dish option.

Directions:

1. Combine the salt, sugar and vinegar in a bowl and add the greens. Toss to evenly coat the greens with the liquid mixture and transfer into the steam rack.
2. Combine together the stock, onions, garlic, oil, and tomato puree in the inner cooking pot and place it in the pressure cooker. Place the steam rack in the pressure cooker with the greens.
3. Close and lock the lid securely and position the steam release handle to sealing position. Pressure cook on high for 10 minutes.
4. When the pressure cooker has completed the cooking cycle, quick release the pressure and wait until the float valve drops down. Open the lid, transfer the greens to the inner cooking pot and let it stand for 10 minutes. Toss the greens with the sauce until evenly coated.
5. Transfer the greens to a serving dish or bowl and pour over the extra sauce. Serve warm.

Ingredients:

- 1 bunch packed fresh collard greens, washed, trimmed and cut into small portions
- ½ cup of chicken stock
- 2 tablespoons of extra virgin olive oil
- ¼ cup of tomato puree
- 1 red onion, halved and thinly sliced
- ½ tablespoon of minced garlic
- 1 tablespoon of red wine vinegar
- ½ teaspoon of salt
- 1 teaspoon of sugar

Preparation time: **30** minutes
Cooking time: **20** minutes
Serves: **4**

CREAMY MASHED POTATOES

Many times when people crave mashed potatoes, they turn to boxed potatoes on weeknights because of the time it takes to cook the potatoes. With the pressure cooker, potatoes can be prepared quickly and easily, making these creamy mashed potatoes a no brainer for your weeknight meal planning.

Directions:

1. Add the stock to the inner cooking pot of the pressure cooker, place in the steam rack and add the potatoes. Close and lock the lid securely and then position the steam release handle to sealing position. Pressure cook on high for 6 to 7 minutes. Quick release the pressure and wait until the float valve drops down.
2. Remove the potatoes, let cool and transfer into a food processor. Add the milk and butter and pulse until smooth and creamy.
3. Season to taste with salt and pepper, transfer into a serving bowl and serve immediately.

Ingredients:

- 2 pounds of potatoes, peeled and cubed
- 1 cup of chicken stock
- ½ cup of milk
- ¼ cup of unsalted butter
- Salt and black pepper, to taste

Preparation time: 15 minutes
Cooking time: 10 minutes
Serves: 4 to 6

BOK CHOI OR CHINESE CABBAGE

Bok choi is a tasty tiny Chinese cabbage. It is simple to prepare in the pressure cooker so if you've never had bok choi, this is a great way to try it. Season with olive oil, salt and pepper or play around with your favorite spice mix.

Directions:

1. Add the bok choi in the inner cooking pot and pour with stock to cover. Season with salt and pepper, and then close and lock the lid securely.
2. Position the steam release handle to sealing position and pressure cook on high for 7 minutes.
3. When the pressure cooker has completed the cooking cycle, quick release the pressure and wait until the float valve drops down. Open the lid, remove the bok choi and toss with oil and salt.
4. Transfer to a serving dish and serve immediately.

Ingredients:

- 1 medium head of fresh bok choi, base trimmed
- 1 cup of stock, or as needed
- Salt and pepper, to taste
- Olive oil, for serving

Preparation time: 5 minutes
Cooking time: 10 minutes
Serves: 3 to 4

SOUTHERN CABBAGE

With butter and bacon you know this dish is from the south! Cabbage holds up well to pressure cooking and makes it a great choice when you want to use the Instant Pot® to prepare your side dish. Season with salt and pepper or your favorite seasonings before serving.

Directions:

1. Add the bacon to the inner cooking pot and press the sauté button. Cook the bacon until lightly browned, stir in the butter, cabbage and the stock. Season to taste with salt and pepper, and then close and lock the lid securely.
2. Position the steam release handle to sealing position and pressure cook on high for 5 minutes using the manual button.
3. When the pressure cooker has completed the cooking cycle, quick release the pressure and wait until the float valve drops down. Open the lid and stir to combine.
4. Transfer to a serving platter and serve warm.

Ingredients:

- 1 medium head of cabbage, base trimmed, and quartered
- ¼ cup diced bacon
- 3 tablespoons of butter
- 2 cups of vegetable or chicken stock

Preparation time: 10 minutes
Cooking time: 15 minutes
Serves: 3 to 4

EGGPLANT WITH OLIVE SPREAD

This Mediterranean inspired dish takes a little time to prepare but is delectable and impressive as either an appetizer or a side dish. I love eggplant and the dip has a wonderful, tangy flavor.

Directions:

1. Add the oil into the inner cooking pot and press the sauté button. Once the oil is hot, fry the eggplants in batches until both sides are lightly browned. When all of the eggplants are browned, add the garlic, stock and season with salt. Close and lock the lid securely and position the steam release handle to sealing position. Press the manual button and cook on high for 3 minutes.
2. When the pressure cooker has completed the cooking cycle, quick release the pressure and wait until the float valve drops down. Remove the garlic and peel, remove the eggplant and transfer into a serving platter.
3. Place the peeled garlic in a blender together with the lemon juice, tahini sauce, olives and thyme leaves and then pulse until smooth.
4. Drizzle the olive sauce on the eggplant and serve immediately.

Ingredients:

- ¼ cup of extra virgin olive oil
- 2 pounds of fresh eggplant, peeled lengthwise, with alternating sections of skin on and off and cut into slices
- 4 crushed and garlic cloves
- 1 teaspoon of table salt
- 1 cup vegetable stock
- 2 tablespoons of lemon juice
- 1 to 2 tablespoons tahini sauce
- 3 tablespoons of pitted black olives
- 1 tablespoon of mince fresh thyme leaves
- Olive oil, for serving

Preparation time: 15 minutes
Cooking time: 15 minutes
Serves: 4 to 6

CHEESY ITALIAN POTATOES

This one is sure to make everyone at the table happy. The Italian seasoning makes magic when mixed with the potatoes, but then you also top them with Parmesan cheese. Voilà! Amazing potatoes!

Directions:

1. Add the butter into the inner cooking pot and press the sauté button. When the butter has melted, sauté the potatoes until the edges are lightly browned or for about 5 minutes. Pour in the stock and then add the seasoning mix and a pinch of salt.
2. Close and lock the lid securely and position the steam release handle to sealing position. Press manual button and pressure cook on high for 12 minutes.
3. When the pressure cooker has completed the cooking cycle, quick release the pressure until the float valve drops down before opening the lid.
4. Transfer the potatoes onto a serving dish and serve immediately with grated Parmesan on top.

Ingredients:

- 1 pound of red potatoes, cubed or quartered
- 2 tablespoons of unsalted butter
- 1 cup of chicken stock
- 1 tablespoon of Italian seasoning mix
- Salt, to taste
- ½ cup of Parmesan cheese, grated

Preparation time: 10 minutes
Cooking time: 20 minutes
Serves: 4

TOMATO STEWED GREEN BEANS

By steaming the beans, you insure that they don't become mushy, but still get the full benefit of being cooked with the tomatoes. I love the flavor in this recipe and hope you will too!

Directions:

1. Coat the inner cooking pot with oil and press the sauté button. When the oil is hot, sauté the garlic for 2-3 minutes or until lightly golden. Stir in the tomatoes with its juices and cook for 4 minutes while stirring regularly.
2. Place the green beans in the steam rack and lightly sprinkle with salt. Transfer the steam rack into the inner pot and then close and lock the lid securely. Press manual button and pressure cook on high for 5 minutes.
3. When the pressure cooker has completed the cooking cycle, quick release the pressure until the float valve drops down. Open the lid and transfer the beans into the inner cooking pot with the tomatoes. Gently toss to coat the beans with the tomato mixture and stir in the basil and 1 teaspoon of olive oil.
4. Transfer the beans and tomato sauce to a serving bowl or dish, and then serve immediately.

Ingredients:

- 1 tablespoon of extra virgin olive oil
- 1 crushed clove of garlic
- 2 cups of canned stewed tomatoes
- 1 pound of fresh green beans, trimmed
- ¼ teaspoon of salt
- 2 tablespoons of chopped fresh basil leaves
- 1 teaspoon of olive oil, or as needed for serving

Preparation time: 5 minutes
Cooking time: 15 minutes
Serves: 3 to 4

Desserts

DULCE DE LECHE

Want to impress your friends? Or maybe your sweet tooth has been working overtime? Whatever the reason, this Dulce de Leche is so incredibly simple to prepare with your Instant Pot®. Plan ahead though, as this must be made a day before you plan to serve it.

Directions:

1. Place the unopened can of condensed milk in the steam rack and place it inside the pressure cooker. Pour enough water to cover the can completely and then close and lock the lid securely.
2. Position the steam release handle to sealing position and pressure cook on high for 20 minutes. Let the pressure release naturally, let it stand in the pressure cooker for 1 hour in keep warm mode and turn the power off. Do not open the lid and leave it in the pressure cooker overnight.
3. On the next day, open the lid and open the can with a can opener. Pour into a serving bowl and serve immediately as a topping or spread.

Ingredients:

- 1 can sweetened condensed milk, unopened with label removed
- Water, as needed

Preparation time: 5 minutes
Cooking time: 25 minutes
Serves: 4

PINA COLADA RICE PUDDING

If you like pina coladas and getting caught in the rain…. Then you will love this rice pudding dessert inspired by the yummy cocktail. Strong coconut flavors mixed with pineapple and rice will having you dreaming of a tropical paradise.

Directions:

1. Combine the rice, water, oil and salt in the inner cooking pot and then close and lock the lid securely.
2. Position the steam release handle to sealing position and press the rice button.
3. While cooking the rice, combine the eggs, evaporated milk and vanilla in a mixing bowl and stir until well combined.
4. When the pressure cooker switches to keep warm mode, quick release the pressure and wait until the float valve drops down. Open the lid and stir in the coconut milk and sugar into the inner pot. Stir in the milk-egg mixture and press the sauté button. Cook until it returns to a boil while stirring regularly.
5. Turn off the pressure cooker and stir in the pineapple. Transfer to a serving bowl and serve with whipped cream and chopped peanuts on top if desired.

Ingredients:

- 1 cup of Italian short-grain rice (Arborio rice)
- 1 ½ cups of coconut water or plain water
- 1 tablespoon of coconut oil
- 2 small pinches of salt
- 2 cups of canned coconut milk
- ½ cup packed raw cane sugar
- 2 medium whole eggs
- ½ cup of evaporated milk
- ½ teaspoon of almond or vanilla extract
- 1 cup of canned pineapple tidbits

Preparation time: 10 minutes
Cooking time: 30 minutes
Serves: 8

LEMON BLACKBERRY CUSTARDS

This is impressive to serve to guests as it looks pretty and tastes sensational! Plus you can have it already made and chilling in the fridge before guests arrive. Use whatever size ramekins you have around and do batches to cook if necessary.

Directions:

1. Mix the egg yolks and sugar in a mixing bowl and whisk until the sugar is completely dissolve. Set aside.
2. In the inner cooking pot of the pressure cooker, add the milk, zest of lemon and the cream and press the sauté button. Bring it to a boil while stirring regularly and press cancel to stop the cooking process. Turn the power off and let it cool completely.
3. When the milk-cream mixture has cooled, gradually pour in the yolk-sugar mixture while whisking constantly until well incorporated.
4. Transfer the mixture into small baking cups or ramekins and cover with foil. Place the steam rack in the pressure cooker and add the baking cups on the rack. Close and lock the lid securely and position the steam release handle to sealing position. Pressure cook on high for 5 minutes.
5. When the pressure cooker has completed the cooking cycle, release the pressure naturally until the float valve drops down. Open the lid, remove the cups and let it rest for 30 minutes to cool completely. Cover the cups with plastic wrap and chill for at least 3 hours before serving.
6. Serve with blackberry syrup and fresh blackberry on top.

Ingredients:

- 1 cup of fresh milk
- 1 cup of full cream
- 6 medium egg yolks
- 1 Lemon, zested
- ½ cup granulated sugar
- Blackberry syrup, for serving
- ½ cup of fresh blackberries

Preparation time: 20 minutes
Cooking time: 20 minutes
Serves: 4 to 6

CHOCOLATE FONDUE

Pressure cooker chocolate fondue is so fun! It will have you wanting to have fondue every night of the week. Serve with fruit, cookies, marshmallows…the options are endless!

Directions:

1. Place the chocolate in heat-proof container and stir in equal amount of cream and sugar. Place the container on a steam rack and place it into the inner pot of the pressure cooker with 2 cups of water.
2. Close and lock the lid securely and position the steam release handle to sealing position. Pressure cook on high for 2 minutes and quick release the pressure until the pressure is released completely. Open the lid and remove the steam rack with a cloth.
3. Stir the mixture thoroughly until well combined and serve immediately with choice of fruit or cookies.

Ingredients:

- ¼ pound of dark bittersweet chocolate, cubed
- ½ cup cream
- ½ tablespoon of sugar

Preparation time: 3 minutes
Cooking time: 5 minutes
Serves: 2

EASY HAZELNUT FLAN

Make this for guests or when you just feel like treating yourself! Even flan will cook up perfectly in the pressure cooker! You can cook the flan in batches or build layers by adding another rack in your pressure cooker.

Directions:

1. Combine together the whole eggs, yolks and sugar in a bowl and whisk until the sugar is completely dissolved. Add caramel sauce on each custard cup just to cover the bottom part and set aside.
2. Add the milk in the inner cooking pot of the pressure cooker and press the sauté button. Heat the milk until it starts to bubble, turn off the pressure cooker and gradually stir in the egg mixture while whisking regularly. Whisk in the cream, hazelnut syrup and vanilla extract in the milk-egg mixture and then pour into the prepared custard cups. Wrap with foil and place it on the steam rack.
3. Add 2 cups of water into the inner cooking pot of the pressure cooker and place the steam rack in the pressure cooker. Close and lock the lid securely and position the steam release handle to sealing position. Pressure cook on high for 6 minutes and release the pressure using the natural release method until the float drops down.
4. Open the lid and carefully remove the steam rack with a cloth. Let the custard rest for 30 minutes, cover with plastic wrap and chill for at least 3 hours before serving.
5. Serve custard with extra whipped cream and chopped hazelnuts if desired.

Ingredients:

- 1 cup of salted caramel sauce

For the Custard
- 3 medium whole eggs
- 2 medium egg yellows
- ¼ cup of white sugar
- 2 cups of fresh milk
- ½ cup of whipped cream
- ½ teaspoon of vanilla/almond extract
- 4 to 5 teaspoons of hazelnut syrup

Preparation time: 5 minutes
Cooking time: 10 minutes
Serves: 4 to 6

BLUEBERRY PUDDING

Our neighbor has dozens of huge blueberry bushes, so when the berries are ripe we usually get a huge bucket of fresh berries. We love to make this blueberry pudding with our fresh berries as a special treat for after dinner.

Directions:

1. Lightly coat a pudding mold that fits in the steam rack with butter and set aside.
2. Mix together the flour, salt and baking powder in a mixing bowl until well combined and then mix in the butter, breadcrumbs and sugar. Add in the milk and egg and mix thoroughly until well incorporated. Fold in the blueberries and stir.
3. Pour the mixture into the prepared pudding mold and fill up to ¾ full. Let it stand for 30 minutes to rise.
4. Pour 2 cups of water in the inner cooking pot and place the steam rack in the pressure cooker. Cover the pudding mold with foil and place it on the steam rack. Close and lock the lid securely and position the steam release handle to sealing position. Pressure cook on high for 15 minutes and leave it in keep warm mode for another 15 minutes.
5. Open the lid when the float valve drops down, remove the pudding by slicing around the sides and transfer to a serving plate.
6. Serve warm with cream.

Ingredients:

- 1 cup of all-purpose sifted flour
- ½ teaspoon of baking powder
- ½ teaspoon of table salt
- ½ cup of cubed unsalted butter
- 2 tablespoons of breadcrumbs
- ½ cup packed white sugar
- 1 medium whole egg, lightly beaten
- ½ cup of milk
- 1 cup of fresh blueberries
- Whipped cream, for serving

Preparation time: 40 minutes (30 minutes allowing to rise)
Cooking time: 30 minutes
Serves: 6

CHEESECAKE

I am a cheesecake addict! Use a 7 inch pan (or anything that you have that will fit in your pressure cooker). I like to use chocolate graham crackers, but that's just because I am a chocoholic. Serve with berries, topping of your choice or enjoy it just as it is!

Directions:

1. Prepare a foil sling by folding a foil into a long ½ inch wide foil sling. This is for easier lifting of the pan from the pressure cooker. Set aside.
2. Add the cream cheese and sugar to a food processor and pulse until smooth. Gradually add the eggs and then the sour cream while processing the ingredients. Add the flour slowly while processing the mixture and then add the vanilla. Process the ingredients for 1 minute, transfer to a bowl and set aside.
3. Combine together the crushed cereal or crackers and melted butter in a separate bowl and mix until they are evenly coated with the butter. Transfer into a round baking pan that fits inside the inner pot and press down to the bottom.
4. Add the cream cheese mixture into the prepared baking pan and cover with foil. Close and lock the lid securely and position the steam release handle to sealing position. Pressure cook on high for 25 minutes.
5. When the Instant Pot® has completed the cooking cycle, use the natural release method in releasing the pressure until the float valve drops down. Open the lid, remove the pan carefully, let it rest for an hour and then chill for at least 6 hours before serving.

Ingredients:

For the Crust
- 1 cup of crushed cereal or graham crackers
- ¼ cup of melted unsalted butter

For the Cheesecake
- 2 cups of cream cheese
- ½ cup packed white sugar
- 2 medium whole eggs
- 3 tablespoons of sour cream
- 2 tablespoons of sifted flour
- ½ teaspoon of vanilla or almond extract

Preparation time: 10 minutes
Cooking time: 25 minutes
Serves: 6

CREME BRULEE

This recipe requires a kitchen torch, or small propane torch of some sort, but it is so worth it. A good creme brûlée is as impressive as it is delicious. If you've never had the crunchy, caramelized sugar melt into your mouth, you are in for a real treat. It is really an easy dessert to prepare, but it's sure to dazzle your diners.

Directions:

1. Add all ingredients except for the superfine sugar to a mixing bowl and mix until well incorporated and smooth.
2. Carefully scoop mixture into six custard cups and cover with foil.
3. Prepare the pressure cooker by adding 1 1/2 cups of water to the inner pot and adding a trivet. Place custard bowls on the trivet, adding another trivet or the steam rack to create a second tier for the remainder of the bowls.
4. Close and lock the lid securely and position the steam release handle to sealing position. Pressure cook on high for 6 minutes. When timer goes off, allow the dessert to sit in pressure cooker for another 10 minutes before doing a quick release of the pressure. Wait until float valve drops to carefully remove the lid and the custard bowls.
5. Allow custard bowls to cool on a wire rack for a minimum of 2 hours.
6. When ready to serve, top each bowl with a tablespoon of superfine sugar and gently shake bowl so that the sugar coats the entire top of the custard. Use a kitchen torch a few inches above the surface to melt the sugar and create a crunchy, caramelized shell.

Ingredients:

- 1 1/2 teaspoons vanilla
- 8 egg yolks
- 1/3 cup sugar
- pinch of salt
- 2 cups of heavy cream
- 6 tablespoons superfine sugar (for before serving) *Superfine sugar may be purchased at many groceries or made at home by blending regular sugar in a food processor until it becomes a very fine consistency.*

Preparation time: 10 minutes
Cooking time: 16 minutes
Serves: 6

FUDGY BROWNIES

Fudgy brownies… To me, there is no better dessert on earth. Even among the fanciest desserts, the brownie will always be my pick. I like to use a hefty amount of chocolate chips for added chocolate yumminess, but feel free to add walnuts, or get crazy and add both!

Directions:

1. Combine together the melted butter and cocoa in a bowl and mix until well combined. Lightly grease a heat-proof pan that fits in the steam rack and set aside.
2. In a separate mixing bowl, combine together the flour, sugar, baking powder and salt and mix until well combined. Mix in the honey, eggs, chopped walnuts and the cocoa-butter mixture and mix until well incorporated.
3. Pour the batter into the prepared pan and cover with foil. Add 2 cups of water into the inner cooking pot and add the steam rack into the pressure cooker. Place the pan with batter on the steam rack, and then close and lock the lid securely.
4. Position the steam release handle to sealing position and pressure cook on high for 35 minutes. Quick release the pressure until the float valve drops down before opening the lid. Serve immediately or chill overnight before serving.

Ingredients:

- 1/2 cup of unsalted butter, melted
- 3 tablespoons of cocoa powder
- 1 cup packed raw cane sugar
- ¾ cup of sifted flour
- ½ teaspoon of baking powder
- 2 small pinches of salt
- 2 to 3 teaspoons of honey
- 2 medium eggs
- ½ cup of chopped walnuts and/ or chocolate chips

Preparation time: 10 minutes
Cooking time: 35 minutes
Serves: 6

LEMON CHEESECAKE

I like to make a lemon cheesecake in the summer when things are just ridiculously hot and we need something refreshing. This cheesecake always does the trick. And by using the pressure cooker, I don't even have to heat up the house by using the oven.

Directions:

1. Prepare a foil sling for lifting the pan out of the pressure cooker by taking an 18" strip of foil and folding it twice lengthwise. Set aside.
2. Combine together the melted butter and crushed grahams in a mixing bowl and mix until well combined. Lightly coat a pan that fits in the steam rack with butter and add the crust mixture. Press down the mixture to the bottom of the entire pan and set aside.
3. Combine together the cream cheese, sugar, sour cream, vanilla, lemon juice and zest and mix until well combined. Mix in the eggs and lightly stir just to incorporate the ingredients together. Pour the batter mixture into the prepared pan and cover with foil.
4. Pour 2 cups of water into the inner cooking pot and place the steam rack and foil sling in the pressure cooker. Place the pan on the steam rack and then close and lock the lid securely. Position the steam release handle to sealing position and pressure cook on high for 25 minutes.
5. When the Instant Pot® has completed the cooking cycle, quick release the pressure until the float valve drops down. Open the lid, remove the pan and let it rest to cool. Cover with plastic wrap and chill for at least 4 hours before serving.

Ingredients:

Crust
- 1 cup of crushed graham crackers or cookies
- 3 tablespoons of melted butter

For the Filling
- 2 cups of cream cheese
- ½ cup packed sugar
- 3 to 4 tablespoons of sour cream
- 1 tablespoon of lemon juice
- ½ lemon, zested
- ½ teaspoon of vanilla or almond extract
- 2 large eggs

Preparation time: 10 minutes
Cooking time: 25 minutes
Serves: 6 to 8